PURPOSEFUL PATHWAYS

Helping Students Achieve Key Learning Outcomes

BY ANDREA LESKES AND ROSS MILLER

PUBLICATIONS IN AAC&U'S GREATER EXPECTATIONS SERIES

 *Association
of American
Colleges and
Universities*

1818 R Street, NW, Washington, DC 20009-1604

Copyright © 2006 by the Association of American Colleges and Universities.
All rights reserved.

ISBN 0-9779210-3-4
To order additional copies of this publication or to find out more about other AAC&U
publications, visit www.aacu.org, e-mail pub_desk@aacu.org, or call 202.387.3760.

The work on which this monograph is based was supported by the Pew Charitable
Trusts and Carnegie Corporation of New York. The publication was made possible
by a grant from Carnegie Corporation of New York. The statements made and views
expressed are solely the responsibility of the authors.

Contents

Acknowledgments

MANY INDIVIDUALS CONTRIBUTED TO THE WORK OF THE GREATER EXPECTATIONS FORUM ON TWENTY-FIRST-CENTURY LIBERAL ARTS EDUCATION PRACTICE on which this publication is based. Carol Geary Schneider, president of the Association of American Colleges and Universities (AAC&U), was the intellectual force behind the creation of the entire Greater Expectations initiative. Barbara Hill, for several years a senior fellow in AAC&U's Office of Education and Quality Initiatives, helped direct the forum. AAC&U staff members and senior fellows led each of the four working groups: Debra Humphreys and Ross Miller (integration), Robert Shoenberg (inquiry), Barbara Hill (global), and Caryn McTighe Musil and Heather Wathington (civic). All of these individuals dedicated precious hours to advancing conversations, conducting meetings, and collecting examples.

The other members of the four working groups, listed on page 69, also deserve recognition for their insights, expertise, and commitment over the course of fourteen months. Hundreds of attendees at the fifteen regional seminars held in 2002 and 2003 greatly enriched our understanding of campus and school practices. Their contributions grounded all of our work in direct action and inspired us throughout the project. Hopefully, these colleagues find we have retained the key aspects of their programs in our descriptions. We regret, however, that space limitations did not permit us to include a larger number of examples. Each reflective seminar took place on a campus; we wish to thank these institutions for their generous contributions-in-kind and acknowledge the invaluable assistance of the local hosts who also helped identify participants and issue invitations.

Deborah Yarrow, Kathleen Fleck, Sally Clarke, and Nancy O'Neill provided invaluable assistance in organizing a seemingly endless number of meetings. At the end of the long process to compile and shape the four working group reports into a final manuscript, Gretchen Sauvey and David Tritelli helped with the editing and Shelley Johnson Carey with the publication process.

The extensive Greater Expectations work would not have been possible without the generous financial support of our two funders, the Pew Charitable Trusts and Carnegie Corporation of New York. A special thank you goes to our program officer, Daniel Fallon, and his colleagues at the Carnegie Corporation for their forbearance. We trust they find their patience justly rewarded.

To all these colleagues, and others involved in the complex endeavors of the forum, our deep appreciation and thanks.

Andrea Leskes

Vice President for Education and Quality Initiatives, AAC&U

Director, Greater Expectations

Ross Miller

Director of Programs

Office of Education and Quality Initiatives, AAC&U

Executive Summary

*T*HERE IS AN EMERGING CONSENSUS AMONG MANY STAKEHOLDERS concerning the important outcomes of a college education for the twenty-first century. This report examines findings of the Greater Expectations Forum on Twenty-First-Century Liberal Arts Education Practice in four of these outcomes:

- integrative learning
- inquiry learning
- global learning
- civic learning

Each represents a complex set of behaviors and knowledge that can best be developed through intentional educational practice from high school through college.

The forum's work sheds light on ways to organize a contemporary liberal education, from school through college, so that all students achieve these outcomes. The report addresses

- definitions of outcomes;
- practices used in both high schools and colleges to advance learning in all four outcomes;
- existing and hypothetical curricular pathways that illustrate how longitudinal growth in the outcomes can be achieved;
- examples of current campus assessment procedures in the four outcomes.

The four outcomes also correlate with the Greater Expectations concept of the intentional student who is empowered (inquiry learning), informed (global learning), and responsible (civic learning). An overarching characteristic of the intentional student is integrative ability.

These findings offer models for high schools and campuses working on local programs in one or more of the outcomes to learn from or adapt. Discussion of the intertwined nature of learning in the four outcomes shows how an intentional approach to planning can create instructional and curricular efficiencies for achieving these outcomes. For example, all four outcomes

- require critical questioning;
- draw upon multiple resources or perspectives to guide thinking and action;
- can involve complex problem solving and application to "real world" issues;

- require acknowledging, grappling with, and probing into differences (be they in disciplines, cultures, social groups, research results, etc.).

Four working groups comprised the forum, one for each outcome. The groups' thirty-four members gathered examples from high school and college practitioners across the country of how to foster student achievement of the four outcomes. Research has shown that learning occurs most effectively when ideas and knowledge are reinforced in a variety of environments and so the forum working groups particularly looked for pathways to advance learning in a cumulative manner, over time, across courses, and across the high school–college boundary. The authors, both AAC&U staff members, expanded on the forum's findings, identifying and describing programs that served to fill perceived gaps in the pathways to high achievement in the outcomes.

The forum confirmed strong interest in the four outcomes and defined each richly. However, individual institutions both described and advanced the outcomes in their own unique ways, reflective of mission, student body, and history. Nonetheless, a set of eight educational practices was often identified as particularly effective, sometimes to advance more than one of the outcomes. These recommended practices include

- learning communities;
- first-year experiences;
- senior capstones and culminating experiences;
- service learning;
- experiential learning;
- authentic tasks (such as collaborative projects, student research, and creative projects);
- problem-based learning;
- interdisciplinary instruction.

Curricular design elements received more attention than pedagogical approaches. True intentional use of the practices, however, to maximize their impact on the desired learning, was still uncommon.

With several notable exceptions, the forum discovered few purposeful pathways throughout the college years that draw together both general education and the majors and almost none that bridged high school and college. Rather, the forum uncovered "faint trails" that only hint at what might emerge in the future. Nor did the forum find a clear developmental understanding of learning from novice to expert in the outcomes or a set of progressive tasks. However, the instructional practices did challenge students at high cognitive levels and elicit deep student effort.

Assessment remains the most underdeveloped step in the teaching and learning cycle and, when in place, tends to be at the experiential input level (did students take part in an activity?) rather than based on direct evidence of learning. The authors supplemented the work of the forum to expand the number of high-level, analytical assessments tailored to the outcomes under examination.

Innovative examples surfaced at campuses and high schools and in projects of all types. Some included elements of learning pathways; a number of these—the best exemplars— address three or four of the outcomes simultaneously. Other isolated but inventive practices have been assembled into hypothetical plans for learning, starting in high school and culminating in college senior-level work. The resulting constructs illustrate how colleges and universities, working in collaboration with the secondary sector, can design programs that powerfully and sequentially help students become better integrative, inquiry, global, and civic learners. ∎

CHAPTER I

The Context and Concepts

*T*HIS MONOGRAPH PRESENTS A RANGE OF PROMISING CURRICULAR AND PEDAGOGIC PRACTICES AT THE HIGH SCHOOL AND COLLEGE LEVELS designed to encourage four sophisticated outcomes of college learning. Its goal is to assist individual campuses and their faculties in strengthening undergraduate student achievement by bringing a greater degree of intentionality to course, curricular, and program design. The publication also encourages alignment of school- and college-level study so that students' learning can deepen over time, through repeated exposure to material at increasingly advanced levels.

Purposeful Pathways: Helping Students Achieve Key Learning Outcomes is based upon the work of the Greater Expectations Forum on Twenty-First-Century Liberal Arts Education Practice. Led by the Association of American Colleges and Universities (AAC&U), Greater Expectations: The Commitment to Quality as a Nation Goes to College was a multi-project initiative to articulate the aims of a twenty-first-century college education and to identify practices that help all undergraduate students achieve those aims. The forum was one in the Greater Expectations family of projects.

The work of the forum related directly to and paralleled the report released in September 2002 by the Greater Expectations national panel. The panel, charged with examining the current context for undergraduate education and formulating a statement of purposes, included the diverse viewpoints of leaders in higher and secondary education, public policy, business, and community action. In its report *Greater Expectations: A New Vision for Learning as a Nation Goes to College* (AAC&U 2002), the panel articulated clearly the kind of learning students need for a constantly changing, interconnected world: a practical, engaged liberal education to prepare them for work, life, and responsible citizenship.

The Intentional Learner

Greater Expectations strongly recommends a powerful core of knowledge and capacities all students should acquire, regardless of background, field of concentration, or chosen higher education institution. In the broadest sense, as a result of this education, students become intentional learners, self-aware about the reasons for their studies, adaptable in using knowledge, and able to connect seemingly disparate experiences. More specifically, to thrive in a complex world, intentional learners become

- *empowered* through the mastery of intellectual and practical skills;
- *informed* by knowledge about and forms of inquiry from the natural and social worlds;
- *responsible* for their personal actions and for civic values.

Taken together, these outcomes form the core of a contemporary liberal education— liberal not in any political sense, but in terms of liberating and opening the mind, and of preparing students for responsible action. *Greater Expectations* suggests that these broad goals for liberal learning become the shared concern of both high schools and colleges, with particular joint attention to the transition from secondary to higher education.

Further support for these goals is apparent in the growing consensus among regional accrediting agencies, specialized disciplinary accreditors, employers, and other stake-holders that the goals of liberal education form a body of essential outcomes of critical importance to all students. (See *Taking Responsibility for the Quality of the Baccalaureate Degree* [AAC&U 2004], a publication of the Greater Expectations Project on Accredita-tion and Assessment.) These goals need to be explicitly addressed throughout the college curriculum: in general education, electives, and the major, as well as in the cocurriculum and in off-campus programs. The learning outcomes are so complex that they can be achieved only when all parts of the educational experience address them in a coordinated manner. In this spirit, the Greater Expectations report urges an end to the traditional, artificial distinctions between liberal and preprofessional education; it envisions a liberal education that is also practical and engaged.

Learning Outcomes for the Twenty-first Century

Drawn from the report's recommendations of specific learning outcomes for all students attending college, this monograph, filled with examples of promising practices, focuses on four major outcomes:

- *Integrative learning* (the ability to connect knowledge across fields, experiences, and levels) is a central characteristic of the intentional learner.
- *Inquiry learning* (the ability to formulate and answer complex questions) is a vital tool of the empowered learner.
- *Global learning* (the ability to understand and find interrelations among the world's communities) is a resource for the informed learner.

INTENTIONAL LEARNERS

Intentional learners are prepared to thrive in a complex, interdependent, diverse, and constantly changing world. Ready to adapt to new environments and integrate knowledge from various sources, they will continue learning throughout their lives.

SUCH LEARNERS ARE
EMPOWERED through
- communication skills
- analytical and problem-solving skills
- information literacy
- strong powers of observation, judgment, and action
- intellectual agility
- creativity
- teamwork and consensus-building skills

INFORMED through
- broad and deep knowledge from many fields
- familiarity with various modes of inquiry
- experience with the human imagination and its artifacts
- understanding of the world's cultures
- knowledge of science and technology
- familiarity with the histories underlying U.S. democracy

RESPONSIBLE for their personal and civic values through
- intellectual honesty
- ethical action
- a commitment to social justice
- an understanding of self and respect for others
- active participation in civic life.

Adapted from *Greater Expectations: A New Vision for Learning as a Nation Goes to College* (AAC&U 2002, 21–24).

- *Civic learning* (the ability to understand and participate in decisions that shape and influence a diverse democratic society) is a fundamental foundation for the responsible learner.

Greater Expectations rightly envisions these abilities as linked. Indeed, examples of good curricular and pedagogical practice may overlap or advance several outcomes simultaneously; the effectiveness of liberal education is in its entirety, not in any discrete part. This publication provides ideas and resources for faculty to shape programs and teaching practices in ways that will begin a comprehensive improvement of learning.

Gathering Promising Practices: The Process

With grant funding from Carnegie Corporation of New York and the Pew Charitable Trusts, AAC&U senior staff members created four working groups, one for each selected outcome. Composed of seasoned researchers and practitioners, these groups each held up to four geographically dispersed meetings to learn about promising practices in program design, pedagogy, administrative structures, and assessment.[1] High school teachers, college faculty members, and administrators were invited to these "reflective seminars" in groups of up to twenty-five. Together they discovered what the secondary and higher education communities are doing to foster intentional learning of the four outcomes. The examples described in chapters 5 and 6 represent a variety of approaches, models, and institutions; some were selected from the rich array shared at the reflective seminars; others came to the notice of the authors through AAC&U's ongoing work.

Attention to promising practices is pertinent at the moment because the knowledge explosion of the last half-century has challenged higher education to provide *all* students with the ability to handle a greatly expanded quantity of information. The needs of businesses and communities for knowledgeable and skilled graduates reinforce the pressure. At the same time, as a result of the larger numbers of students in college and their diverse levels of preparation, campuses must help a wider range of students to learn better, no matter their readiness. Fortunately, the scholarship of learning offers guidance on how to proceed. To quote Lion Gardiner,

> Research on student development, coupled with modern educational methods and quality improvement principles, *can enable us for the first time in human history to educate all of the people to a high level.* We will, however, have to use, rather than ignore, research. (1994, vii)

The Greater Expectations recommendations to improve learning stress the interconnected concepts of "intentionality" and "coherence." Intentionality refers to an alignment of action with desired aims. In the Greater Expectations vision—called the New Academy— the aims include educating students to become intentional learners who are empowered,

---

[1] The working group members and their affiliations at the time of the project are listed on page 69.

informed, and responsible. Some of the actions to align, and the ones emphasized in this publication, include the architectural design of the curriculum, teaching methods, and assessments. Coherence implies a logical sequence of coursework or of educational experiences to foster cumulative learning over time, beyond the confines of a single course. This is not a prescription that dictates exactly how teaching and learning should occur in each and every course but rather what Jim Ratcliff (1997) calls a "conscious design for learning." Coherence also implies that the faculty collectively reflects upon how courses and experiences fit together and interrelate—from the student perspective—to create explicit learning plans. In *Greater Expectations*, such learning plans that exhibit both intentionality and coherence are called "purposeful pathways."

Intentional Practice and Purposeful Pathways

To achieve intentional educational practice, at a minimum institutions need to put in place

- clear goals and outcomes for student learning;
- curricular design and pedagogical practices related to the outcomes and planned so as to advance their attainment;
- authentic assessment derived, first, from the outcomes and, second, from the actual work faculty ask students to undertake.

A powerful cycle of improvement is created when these elements are thoughtfully implemented and data are gathered to inform revisions. The graphic below, reproduced from *Taking Responsibility for the Quality of the Baccalaureate Degree* (AAC&U 2004), illustrates the improvement cycle.

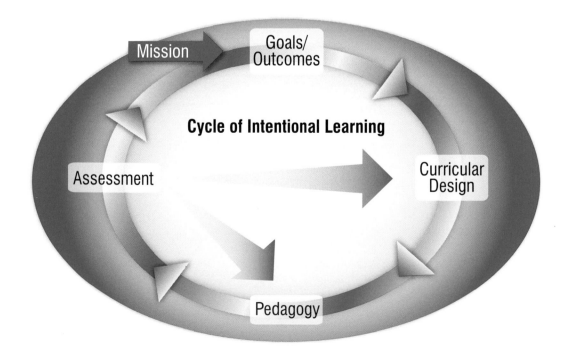

Student engagement with higher-order cognition (e.g., application, analysis, and synthesis) arises from the rich activities that comprise instruction in the four learning outcomes selected for attention by the Greater Expectations forum. Integrative, inquiry, global, and civic learning can move students toward deeper thinking, critical analysis, creative transfer of knowledge, and tolerance for ambiguity. Purposeful pathways that advance such learning to sophisticated levels will contribute importantly to the ultimate goal of educating all students now attending college for the complexities of the contemporary world.

To be more explicit, purposeful pathways are designed sequences of courses or experiences, created by the faculty, that lead students to high levels of learning, intellectual skill development, and practical knowledge. They are plans that provide students with multiple opportunities to put specific knowledge and skills to use; each such opportunity relates to and builds on the previous ones. Purposeful pathways for the broad outcomes of liberal learning utilize many strategies—general education courses, modules, major requirements, cocurricular experiences, off-campus learning—gaining power through careful management of the interrelationships among the elements.

King's College in Wilkes-Barre, Pennsylvania, offers some of the best designs for purposeful pathways in use on campuses. The following abridged example illustrates a pathway that incorporates a module, a general education course, and major requirements each contributing in specific and planned ways to the achievement of an important outcome of undergraduate education: information literacy.

A Purposeful Pathway at King's College

One of the transferable skills of liberal learning expected of King's College graduates is *effective use of library and information technology*. For students majoring in marketing, this has been interpreted by the departmental faculty as the ability to plan and implement comprehensive search strategies, use sophisticated forms of information, and employ research techniques appropriate to marketing research.

Examples of...	Competencies	Curricular strategies	Assessment standards
Freshman year	uses important library tools	Core 110: Effective Writing. Module with basic library skills workbook	■ completes with passing grade ■ competent library skills ■ compares and contrasts sources
	uses MLA style of documentation	Core 110. At least one required research paper	■ correctly uses style
Sophomore year	identifies, locates, analyzes, and appropriately uses company, industry, product, and demographic information	Marketing 233: Principles of Marketing. Preparation of a marketing plan	■ appropriately identifies type of information needed ■ validates through other sources ■ synthesizes
Junior/senior year	uses resources related to international marketing	Marketing 243: International Marketing. Preparation of a feasibility study for introducing products into a foreign country	■ uses information to assess cultural, social, political, and economic situation ■ uses data to make a marketing decision
Senior year	designs and implements sophisticated searches to support marketing plan	Marketing 281: Marketing Management. Preparation of a marketing plan at a professional level to introduce a new product	■ synthesizes data from various sources and presents in appropriate formats

Purposeful pathways within institutions depend upon a collective faculty agreement about outcomes and clear articulation of the learning expected at different stages. Across levels, too, most particularly from high school to college, purposeful pathways imply alignment of expectations, content, and teaching methods. Since 75 percent of high school graduates now continue their education (The Education Trust–West 2002), schools need to prepare all students for further study. Students who encounter in high school the kinds of learning they will encounter in college are better prepared to succeed as freshmen. For instance, experience in interdisciplinary work—and reflection on it—in high school will position students well to integrate various perspectives in a multidisciplinary freshman learning community. High school study of global geography and politics will provide a basis for subsequent courses in international affairs or area studies.

Gardiner (1994), as he exhorts educators to make use of the research findings about how people learn, lays a basis for designing purposeful pathways. Higher-order learning, he asserts, develops slowly and needs to be fostered deliberately throughout the college experience. Other researchers agree. In all domains, deep learning and expertise require extensive time and practice (Bransford, Brown, and Cocking 2000); when spaced out, for example over several years, this practice is more effective than when massed together all at once (Halpern and Hakel 2003). In addition, to develop fluent transferability of learning from one context to another, students need to apply their knowledge and skills in varied environments (Halpern and Hakel 2003); if they practice retrieval under a range of learning conditions, they will better develop "multiple retrieval cues" as the learning becomes more "available" in memory. Finally, the higher-order cognitive skills so important to faculty, students, and society require the explicit teaching of ways of thinking, copious practice, and frequent assessment of progress (McKeachie et al. 1990; Woods 1987). Taken together, these findings strongly support the idea of careful, multiyear sequencing of college learning.

Thus, purposeful pathways require intentional design of curricula and pedagogy accompanied by conscious choices among those practices that have been shown to improve learning. Such pathways ensure that learning is not left to chance, but results from planned instruction and skillful effort on the part of both students and teachers. Because no single series of learning experiences will be best for every student or every discipline, creativity and variety in planning and advising will emerge as important factors in fostering greater achievement for all students, no matter their fields of study, prior preparation, or backgrounds.

Intellectual Development and Experiential Levels of Learning

The concept of purposeful pathways resonates well with several theoretical framings of how learning occurs. Although this monograph is designed to be practical rather than conceptual, theory might help validate actions to implement coherent programs that develop learning over time and across the curriculum (in general education courses, in the majors, and in professional studies).

The spiral theory of learning

Bruner (1960), Kolb (1983), Perry (1999), and Kegan (1982) all describe the process of learning using the metaphor of an ascending spiral. A successful learning spiral entails both the expansion of experiences *and* an increasing level of cognitive complexity. During each "turn of the spiral" students engage subjects in multiple ways—through integrating experiences; rigorous reflection; theoretical concepts, models, or perspectives; and active practices or experimentation. Diversity of perspectives, ideas, and contexts is of central importance to rich learning and timely development.

A spiral of learning for a cross-cutting outcome could parallel a learning spiral for disciplinary content. Inquiry activities, for example, could accompany beginning, intermediate, and advanced study of history, with the expectation that the heightened sophistication of the inquiry analyses would match the growing body and complexity of historical knowledge. Through experiences, reflections, theories, and practices—and when subjected to diverse critical viewpoints—both historical knowledge and inquiry ability would be deepened. Such a spiral of learning at the college level would require a faculty collectively to plan for learning over time.

The working group on civic learning developed a similar model, a braided spiral or helix, to describe how students develop civic learning from high school through college as well as within each educational level. The lines braided together represent six elements: self, communities and cultures, knowledge, skills, values, and public action. As the spiral turns, signifying increasingly sophisticated learning, students experience these six elements in more interconnected, integrative ways.

Student intellectual development theory

Following the leads provided by John Dewey and Jean Piaget, psychologists like Bruner (1960), Perry (1999), King and Kitchener (1994), and Belenky et al. (1986) have greatly refined and expanded knowledge of student intellectual development. At the same time, their work increased attention to learning styles, women's ways of knowing, and the implications of student development theory for teaching and learning from high school through college. In his body of work, Piaget recommended that teachers challenge learners with tasks at the next developmental level, slightly higher than their current one. Vygotsky (1978) proposed a somewhat similar concept: the "zone of proximal development." All these ideas can be fruitfully applied to the development of the four cross-cutting liberal learning outcomes over a student's entire education.

Knefelkamp, Widick, and Parker (1978) synthesized and extrapolated from this family of learning and developmental theories, especially those of Dewey and Perry. They suggested matching the challenge and variety of assignments with student developmental levels to stimulate movement upward through the learning spiral. As described by Knefelkamp and Cornfield (1979), well-designed learning can foster change in students' cognitive perceptions of learning and knowing, their ability to learn from peers, their understanding of the student role, their view of good instruction and fair evaluation, and the sources of developmental challenge and support.

Such an approach requires that teachers discover students' intellectual levels and then challenge them appropriately to stimulate their progress. Intellectual complexity as described by Perry (1999) and others identifies several stages: early dualism (learning is understood as the memorization of right answers and facts); a middle stage (learning involves methods and procedures, ways of learning, and ways of knowing to search for new knowledge); and a later stage (knowledge is understood to be constructed and contextual). It must be underscored that intentional development through these levels depends upon insightful instructional planning. If, as one would expect, programs or institutions hold student intellectual maturity as a major goal, then low-level, "delivered" content or knowledge should generally be de-emphasized in favor of more challenging learning experiences, complemented by attention to complexity and diversity.

Faculty and institutional imagination will be needed to create instructional sequences to advance the four outcomes in ways that encourage student progression through the developmental stages. Especially advantageous would be powerful experiences in high school that prepare students to begin college-level work at a stage beyond dualism (or at least primed for such a move). Unfortunately, many instructors tend to be either unaware of (if they never studied psychology or educational theory) or unable to apply (even if they have) the insights about learning inherent in research on learning styles and levels of intellectual complexity. Support for faculty endeavors to assess individual student development and apply the relevant theoretical principles to course and curricular design could help create the needed expertise.

A hierarchy of development in civic learning

Based upon empirical observations of campus work, Musil (2003) proposed six sequential phases or expressions of citizenship achieved through an expanding awareness of the self, community, and values in a civic context. The six phases—exclusionary, oblivious, naive, charitable, reciprocal, and generative—develop from a foundation for civic learning of

- knowledge and reflection about the self and others;
- an integrated understanding of contexts, communities, and inequalities;
- skills in democratic and intercultural competencies;
- an ability to take public action in concert with others for the public good.

At each successive phase, the awareness of community expands and the perspectives increase in sophistication. It is interesting to note the similarity to the "turn of the spiral" elements mentioned earlier, in particular integration, reflection, theory, multiple perspectives, and experimentation.

Successful implementation of such a hierarchical model needs institution-wide definitions of the six phases and broad participation. Understanding the citizenship phases and the means to facilitate learning would require ongoing faculty development for all professors as refinements to program and departmental curricula are made. Through collective analysis and discussion, the faculties on individual campuses could create benchmarks for civic learning or any other selected outcome (the behaviors or other evidence of achievement at increasing levels of awareness). Related rubrics, for example, could score student work according to the behaviors associated with the citizenship phases as described in a statement of standards. ■

CHAPTER 2

Observations

*T*HE FIFTEEN REGIONAL MEETINGS HELD BY THE FOUR FORUM WORKING GROUPS INVOLVED SOME THREE HUNDRED PRACTITIONERS. Without exception, the groups discovered intriguing examples of teaching and learning. As each group summarized and evaluated its findings and the AAC&U staff completed further analysis, several important observations emerged.

The Outcomes

Interest in the four outcomes—integrative, inquiry, global, and civic learning—was and remains strong at individual institutions and across the country. The call for participation in a project on integrative learning jointly sponsored by AAC&U and the Carnegie Foundation for the Advancement of Teaching attracted 140 applications. A very recent project on refocusing general education on global issues attracted eighty-nine.

No dissension exists as to the need for students graduating from college in the twenty-first century to learn through integration and inquiry and be globally aware and civically engaged. While each campus may have its own definition, the differences are not great. Therefore, each outcome can be quite clearly defined or described (see chapter 3). However, each outcome can be fostered and achieved in many ways—the proverbial multiple paths up the mountain—so that the particular practices (or constellation of practices) in place on any one campus will be unique to its mission, student profile, history, culture, and faculty interests. This situation should not be surprising; it is no different for the traditional disciplines or even professional programs (one campus may emphasize the oral dimension of foreign language competency and use an interactive method while another focuses on literature and depends on text-based study). The four outcomes are being developed in highly varied ways, adapted for particular institutions and the students they enroll.

The Educational Practices

A few instructional arrangements, familiar to (if not yet utilized by) many high school and college faculty members, emerged from the regional seminars as offering broad potential to facilitate student learning in several or all of the targeted outcomes. Learning communities, first-year experiences, senior capstones, service learning, experiential learning, authentic tasks (e.g., student research, and creative or collaborative projects), problem-based learning, and interdisciplinary study were among the instructional arrangements common across the outcomes. They are further described in chapter 4 and illustrated in chapter 5.

Intentional use of these eight categories of practices (and others) to advance the desired outcomes—effectively maximizing their potential—is, however, still uncommon. Students might engage in a service-learning experience but without close faculty guidance, integration into classroom study, or reflection on the multiple aspects of civic learning. One can view this widespread situation as a stage in the enterprise-wide crawl toward a more conscious approach to teaching and learning. With these eight practices, as with others, it is through purposeful use that they gain power and utility.

As a general rule, curricular design and ways to organize the student experience received more attention in campus work than classroom teaching and learning; for instance, there are fewer examples of problem-based learning than of learning communities. AAC&U has regularly observed this predilection for curricular reform instead of pedagogy so it was no surprise to encounter it again in this project. However, less expected—but quite satisfying—was an increased interest in pedagogy and how it could interact with and reinforce curricular structures. In excellent examples, students taking a service-learning course or studying abroad also conducted research; within a learning community, teams of students solved real-world problems.

Sequential Learning and Purposeful Pathways

When first designing the Greater Expectations forum, AAC&U hoped that the reflective seminars would reveal both good individual practices and purposeful pathways leading to the selected learning outcomes. Although alignment across the mostly unexamined high school–college boundary was known to be uncommon—although thought to be possible—it was hoped that conscious designs for learning might well appear in those institutions particularly attentive to student learning on either side of that illogical dividing line. However, with a few notable exceptions featured in chapter 5, the regional seminars revealed only "faint trails" hinting at what might in the future become purposeful pathways to ensure widespread intellectual growth in the four selected outcomes of liberal education. For instance, coherent programs (as opposed to assignments or courses) that enhance the ability to integrate across disciplines and contexts were rare; even rarer were those that did so over time and in cumulative ways.

AAC&U President Carol Geary Schneider has described both the existing situation and offered a direction for improvement:

> Any course has multiple aims and must focus simultaneously on content and students' development of important capabilities. Currently the capabilities addressed across a series of courses are . . . often accidental and disconnected. Students may be entirely unaware of them in too many courses. Greater Expectations is proposing that school and college faculty members each begin to map their expectations transparently and developmentally, across successively higher levels of the formal curriculum. (2003, 16)

Analysis also failed to reveal a clear set of progressive tasks in the four outcomes. Similar assignments might appear at the various levels from high school through college (e.g., reflective journaling, design problems) and while individual teachers might expect different standards of performance, little or no coordination of these expectations emerged. Greater knowledge on the part of faculty members about what students can achieve at the novice, intermediate, and expert levels could lead to appropriate standards. Several decades of education reform have shown that student performance is highly influenced by expectations; setting a low bar leads to poor work. Unless and until further practitioner research elucidates developmental sequences, an advanced knowledge of student capacities, careful planning of instruction, and instructor skill in motivating students to learn will be important classroom resources.

To return briefly to the issue of linkages across the high school–college boundary, purposeful pathways of learning—whether general learning outcomes like the ones examined by the forum or traditional disciplinary content—will depend on sustained conversations and collaborations. At the state level, a good example of what can be done resulted from the governor-appointed Wisconsin International Trade Council (WITCO) Taskforce on International Education. After an initial conversation in which a broad group of stakeholders scanned current work and suggested an agenda for action, leaders from the elementary, secondary, and higher education sectors developed a vision statement for collaborative educational efforts to address the state's international needs. The statement stresses how a global curriculum is a K–16 collaborative endeavor in which educators "regularly communicate across disciplines and levels of instruction and work together to provide well-articulated learning experiences for students from their first years of schooling throughout their formal academic careers and beyond as life-long learners."[2] At the individual institutional levels, many colleges and universities have strong partnerships with local high schools; these relationships can form the basis for curricular and pedagogical planning that focuses classroom teachers and college professors on important learning outcomes.

Challenging and Authentic Educational Experiences

The Greater Expectations forum project produced only anecdotal evidence. However, nearly all the instructional practices shared in the regional seminars challenged students at high cognitive levels, generated serious student effort, and motivated student engagement—all consequences of considerable benefit in accomplishing difficult goals. In many cases, students pursued "authentic" work that placed them in situations similar to those encountered by professionals in the field and required the concepts and skills (at an appropriate level of sophistication) that such experts would employ to solve problems. Rigorous, challenging, and authentic educational experiences increase learning; they do so even more effectively when incorporated into cumulative purposeful pathways.

[2] The full statement is available online at www.uw-igs.org/userimages/vision_statement.pdf.

Assessments

In the contexts of the forum's work, the Greater Expectations initiative, and this publication, assessment targets learning improvement. More extensive discussions can be found in three recent AAC&U publications: *The Art and Science of Assessing General Education Outcomes* (Leskes and Wright 2005), *Levels of Assessment: From the Student to the Institution* (Miller and Leskes 2005), and *Our Students' Best Work: A Framework for Accountability Worthy of Our Mission* (AAC&U 2005).

Direct assessment of outcomes is the most underdeveloped step of the teaching and learning cycle, although impressive attention to assessment continues to occupy colleges and universities across the country. All the work of the Greater Expectations forum, with its extensive array of reflective seminars, unearthed few good examples. Attention was mostly focused on experiential input (e.g., requiring students to complete a course or to study abroad) rather than on evidence of learning. When a campus did state an outcome expectation, it was often part of a larger assignment and assessed as part of a checklist of requirements (e.g., requiring that, as one of several criteria for full credit, a student's research paper cite two references addressing global issues). Even when creative faculty members chose learning experiences to promote a specific outcome, procedures and rubrics to assess the level of learning *in the targeted outcome* were often missing. In an assignment designed to promote integrative learning, for example, the assessment would primarily consider disciplinary knowledge, associated communication skills, or participation in required activities. Specific, analytical assessment of the quality of integrative learning (or any of the four outcomes) that resulted from the learning experiences was mostly lacking.

As the authors have insisted elsewhere (Miller and Leskes 2005), assessment of learning rests on analyzing evidence, and the best evidence comes from student work products rather than from an input inventory. This is the case whether the assessment is formative (occurs during and impacts the learning process) or summative (occurs at an endpoint). Further, validity is enhanced when the assessment tool or task closely matches the learning it is designed to measure; an assignment, used for assessment purposes, that asks students to employ perspectives from two disciplines will be a more valid tool for determining integrative learning than one that simply requests a critical analysis. To improve intentionality in assessment, one would also maximize the authenticity of the exercise by assuring a high degree of similarity between the student's task and an expert's actual work in the domain. Finally, authentic work products can be assessed holistically (was it adequate?) or analytically (which particular aspects were satisfactory based on standards and a rating scale?).

With these concepts in mind, one can construct a simple hierarchy of assessment that summarizes the state of the field. The levels are organized by (a) the primary emphasis of the assignment/exercise and (b) the holistic or analytical nature of the assessment.

Assessment Hierarchy

	Description	Example of assignment/exercise
Level 1	Assessment rests on a summary of *inputs*, a confirmation of student *exposure* to the experience.	Did the student take a course that includes assignments or experiences in civic learning?
Level 2	Assessment looks at and evaluates *holistically* work generated for an assignment/exercise of which the desired outcome is a *by-product*.	A collaborative engineering project, of the team's choosing, mentions associated social issues.
Level 3	Assessment looks at and evaluates *holistically* work generated for an assignment/exercise *designed to elicit* the desired outcome.	Was the student's overall performance during a service-learning experience at a community agency of an unacceptable, acceptable, or superior quality?
Level 4	Assessment looks at and evaluates *analytically* work generated for an assignment/exercise of which the desired outcome is a *by-product*.	In addition to the quality of design, did a collaborative engineering project show superior, acceptable, or unacceptable evidence of integrating (1) theory with practice and (2) societal needs with technology?
Level 5	Assessment looks at and evaluates *analytically* work generated for an assignment/exercise *designed to elicit* the desired outcome.	How well did the self-reflection on service learning at a community agency reveal the student's capacity to (1) analyze power relationships, (2) work in a setting with cultural difference, and (3) recognize ethical problems related to working with community clients?

Chapter 6 provides some examples of level 2–5 assessments related to the four outcomes. These examples were gathered to supplement the forum's data set, which unfortunately did not include many sophisticated assessment models. The growing national attention to assessment as a tool for learning improvement—a trend that has been much in evidence recently—most likely accounts for the now richer choice of examples. ■

CHAPTER 3

Defining the Four Outcomes

&DUCATION CAN HAVE MANY WORTHY GOALS, SOME DISCRETE AND EASILY ACHIEVED, OTHERS OVERARCHING AND REQUIRING LONG-TERM EFFORT. Given the limited time and resources for education at all levels, students will feel most rewarded when instruction "pays them back" for their efforts by making subsequent learning and performance better or easier. Jerome Bruner insisted that "learning should serve us in the future" (1960, 17), and the four outcomes examined by the forum clearly have both broad and continuing potential to serve graduates well in a century marked by rapid changes in knowledge, technology, and cross-cultural communication.

The following definitions and explanations of the four outcomes build on the work of the forum. They reflect the existing literature, AAC&U's knowledge of relevant practices, and the personal expertise of the forum's many participants. However, to better reflect particular missions, settings, or resources, individual institutions may choose to refine them. Through both definition and practice, each educational community can explain what the outcomes mean in a local context: examples of the kinds of evidence that best document achievement could be used to clarify the broad definitions of such complex outcomes. An institutional or departmental portfolio, containing student products of both high and lower (but still acceptable) quality, could be used to illustrate local standards.

> *What do you consider to be the end purpose of education? Is it not to bring about an integrated individual?*
>
> –Jiddu Krishnamurti

Integrative Learning – A Central Characteristic of the Intentional Learner

Integrative learning is a process in which learners

- draw on diverse points of view;
- understand issues contextually;
- connect knowledge and skills from multiple sources and experiences;
- adapt learning from one situation to another, applying it in varied settings.

Students who have become integrative learners are able to

- ask pertinent, insightful questions about complex issues as they perceive relations and patterns;
- recognize conflicting points of view and move beyond the conflicts to a personal stance;
- synthesize from different ways of knowing, bodies of knowledge, and tools for learning;
- tolerate ambiguity and paradox;

- reflect constructively on their experiences and knowledge;
- employ confidently a range of intellectual tools;
- tackle and solve practical problems and work through difficult situations;
- connect in- and out-of-classroom work;
- apply theories to practice in the real world;
- balance diverse perspectives in deciding whether to act (in the classroom, workplace, or community);
- distinguish the multiple consequences and implications of their actions.

Integrative learning builds on significant knowledge in individual disciplines and interdisciplines. Experiences that foster integrative learning often take students out of single field-specific contexts and also out of the classroom to address real-world issues. Powerful learning occurs when the problems posed are unscripted, drawn from the outside world, without simple answers, and sufficiently broad to require information from multiple areas of knowledge. In examining ways to reduce rates of HIV/AIDS infection in Africa or boost the economic vitality of the Puget Sound region of Washington State, students may be led to consider politics, economics, history, biology, and other areas of learning. Such problems inherently lend themselves to a range of valid solutions and benefit from varied perspectives.

About Integrative Learning[3]

While education has long been seen as a vehicle to integrate life, learning, passions, and commitments, the challenges of the contemporary world bring a new urgency to the issue of connection and integration. Integrative learning—whether across disciplines or from one environment to another—is clearly important for today's students who, after graduation, will face complex issues in their personal, work, and civic lives. In most fields—from the workplace to scientific discovery to medicine to world and national affairs—multilayered, unscripted problems routinely require integrative thinking and approaches.

AAC&U has long been a strong voice urging higher education to provide students with more opportunities to explore connections across disciplines and with the world beyond the academy (AAC 1991). Connecting ideas, teaching big themes across disciplines, and applying conceptual learning to real-world problems are stressed by stakeholders of all stripes—including, among many others, the federal government (U.S. Department of Education 1998), the Accreditation Board for Engineering and Technology (2000), the Business–Higher Education Forum (1999), and the National Council of Teachers of Mathematics (2000). In *How People Learn*, Bransford, Brown, and Cocking (2000, 139) suggest that in traditional curricula, "though an individual objective might be reasonable, it is not seen as part of a larger network. Yet it is the network, the connections among

[3]This section includes material adapted from the foreword to *Integrative Learning: Mapping the Terrain* (Huber and Hutchings 2004).

objectives, that is important . . . to understand an overall picture that will ensure the development of integrated knowledge."

Given the interest from many sectors and the exciting developments in integrative and interdisciplinary scholarship that are transforming so many fields of study, support for integrative learning appears to be quite strong. The challenge remains, however, to turn promising integrative learning innovations into coherent programs of study with progressively more rigorous expectations.

It is worth just a word here on the conflation of interdisciplinary and integrative learning. To quote from the statement developed jointly by AAC&U and the Carnegie Foundation for the Advancement of Teaching, "integrative learning comes in many varieties. . . . Significant knowledge within individual disciplines serves as the foundation, but integrative learning goes beyond academic boundaries" (Huber and Hutchings 2004, 13). Not all forms of integrative learning are the same, and interdisciplinarity is not synonymous with integration. Interdisciplinary courses and programs, designed to bring different disciplinary perspectives to bear on salient themes or contemporary issues, represent only one pathway to integrative learning; linking theory to practice offers another, as does utilizing diverse and even contradictory points of view within a discipline.

Doubt is an incentive to truth, and patient inquiry leadeth the way.
–Hosea Ballou

Inquiry Learning – A Vital Tool of the Empowered Learner

Inquiry learning is a process in which learners
- seek their own theories, answers, or solutions;
- conduct investigations, building methodological skills in systematic ways;
- gather knowledge as it is needed to pursue lines of questioning typical of experienced practitioners;
- ask questions and investigate issues in ways characteristic of disciplines, thereby learning to think like experts in that field.

Students skilled in inquiry
- go beyond facile answers to engage with the complexity of a situation;
- readily identify ambiguities and unanswered questions;
- understand the differences among—and employ appropriately the critical methods of—analysis, synthesis, and comparison.

An inquiry approach to education asks students to engage actively with both the material studied and the process of learning, thereby assuming responsibility for their own progress. Pedagogies that elicit questioning while sharpening critical thinking and problem-solving skills foster powers of inquiry: observing, gathering data, constructing hypotheses, conducting experiments, designing models, engaging in trial and error, and reasoning precisely.

About Reasoned Inquiry

As far back as Socrates, the ability to engage in reasoned inquiry was the hallmark of an educated person. Whether the object of inquiry was oneself or the world, the capacity to ask and answer questions through investigation, logic, and informed judgment defined intellectual maturity.

The general intellectual skills necessary to function well in the workplace, in civil society, and in multiple private roles have been distilled to a triumvirate of communication, critical analysis, and creativity in dealing with unscripted problems. Developing proficiency in each requires extensive practice of reasoned inquiry and discourse in a variety of contexts.

Learning through inquiry is an active process of "inquiring into," of pursuing answers or solutions on one's own initiative rather than expecting to be presented with them. Inquiry learning, which can operate on any content matter, concerns the process of acquiring knowledge and understanding. For example, in sociology it would involve time spent on asking and investigating questions as a sociologist, making use of sociological facts and theories learned in that process and previously.

Inquiry learning does not set up a dichotomy between process and content, but stresses process as a way of organizing the curriculum and determining pedagogical practices. With attention to the process of inquiry, courses in methodology might come early in the major, be applied in field-specific courses, and lead to a culminating senior research project. Inquiry—whether in the form of research, scholarship, or artistic creation—is the characteristic activity of faculty members and graduate students. A focus on inquiry learning extends the same active engagement to the undergraduate level.

Global Learning – A Resource for the Informed Learner

Global learning is a process by which individuals
  - gain knowledge about the world's cultural diversity and interconnectedness;
  - consider issues and action from the perspectives of many cultures and discover their extended implications;
  - prepare for personal, professional, and civic activity in a world of instant communications, multinational corporations, codependent economies, stark inequalities, intertwined environments, and diasporic cultures.

Globally educated students
  - understand the scientific, historical, geographical, cultural, political, economic, and religious contexts of issues;
  - recognize the similarities and differences among cultures and the identities they engender;

The new electronic interdependence recreates the world in the image of a global village.
—Marshall McLuhan

- link cultural literacy with language learning and actively pursue linguistic competency in languages beyond their own so as to communicate effectively across cultures;
- understand the world's different political systems and the varied ways of practicing democracy;
- develop sophisticated worldviews that enable them to see beyond national citizenship;
- translate knowledge of the world into ethical, reflective practice that keeps in mind the consequences of actions in locally diverse and globally heterogeneous communities;
- recognize the impact both of global issues on individual lives and of individual and collective action on the larger world.

Global learning both develops the skills and provides the contexts for a habit of mind that looks beyond local environments to humanity, writ large. It results from wide-ranging knowledge acquisition and practice; from study and intercultural experiences; and from comprehensive engagement with important cultural, scientific, and societal issues.

About Global Learning

At the present moment in history, global learning has particular urgency. Most major societal issues—whether environmental, economic, or political in nature—cannot be confined within national borders. As Mazur and Sechler (1997, 9) have cogently written,

> In a world made smaller by global commerce and communication, cooperative engagement among nations is more possible—and more necessary—than ever before. "Cooperative engagement," in this context, refers to the complex of policies, programs, treaties, investments, and regimes by which nations collaborate to advance common interests . . . military security, economic growth and trade, and what might be called social stewardship—the promotion of health, social stability, and human potential.

Higher education's concern with internationalization can be traced back to the aftermath of World War II. During the Cold War period, attention to international issues was seen as directly related to the country's national security and international competitiveness. After the political upheavals of the early 1990s in the Soviet Union and Eastern Europe, all aspects of international education assumed a greater economic focus with the expansion of American commercial interests. Increased global migrations, intertwined economic and manufacturing processes, and the ease of rapid international communication and travel have blurred the more traditional national and cultural boundaries which, in turn, have affected how higher education approaches global learning.

At the secondary school level, too, attention to global issues has grown, in part because of the dramatic shift in the demographic profile of students. In the curriculum, it is most clearly reflected within the context of world history (the story of interactions within and among societies over time) and digital telecommunications across borders.

The attention to global learning at all levels of education is timely given that the United States clearly has a need for more specialists in the languages, histories, economics, and politics of the entire globe. For these professionals to be effective, they must be broadly educated about the contexts, cultures, and communities in which their specific skills will be used. Global learning is critical to both individuals and society in an interconnected world and must increasingly be part of a contemporary liberal education.

The current challenge for higher education is to provide today's more diverse students— more diverse racially, ethnically, economically, and in terms of their preparation than their World War II–era counterparts—with opportunities for global learning suited to the twenty-first century. Musil (2006) and Hovland (2006) make the point that, to respond, the academy will need to stretch and reshape its approaches to global learning by thinking more comprehensively and relating global learning to the students' own experiences.

Civic Learning – A Fundamental Foundation for the Responsible Learner

Civic learning helps students

- gain comparative knowledge about diverse individuals and groups of people who have shaped the United States and the larger world;
- acquire the skills to facilitate the collective work of diverse groups to protect life, liberty, equality, and democratic practices and institutions;
- develop the values, discipline, and commitment to pursue responsible public action.

Civically engaged learners

- understand and are able to balance the rights and interests of diverse individuals with the collective needs of a larger, diverse society;
- have the capacity to analyze power relationships, structures of inequality, and social systems that govern individual and communal life;
- are skilled in the arts of democracy and committed to the democratic aspirations of equality, opportunity, inclusion, and justice;
- show concern for others, promote racial/cultural understanding, and are capable of crossing boundaries of difference;
- possess the courage to act, based on the belief that actions make a difference, thereby engaging—individually and in concert with others—in public life to build and sustain democratic institutions.

Never doubt that a small group of committed citizens can change the world; indeed, it's the only thing that ever has.

–Margaret Mead

In the United States, the concept of civic learning derives directly from individual and collective responsibility for maintaining a functioning, inclusive, diverse democracy. Such learning benefits from rich field experiences that complement classroom discussion and analysis. Knowledge derived from many disciplines, perspectives, and cultures contributes to the breadth of learning that anchors wise action.

About Civic Learning

Education from kindergarten through college in the United States has always had both an academic and a civic mission. The nation's schooling system was designed as a major socializing vehicle to produce not simply educated people, but educated citizens. Although the balance between educational and societal obligations has varied over time, with the rise in influence of high-stakes testing for schools and of the research agenda for higher education, any semblance of balance has disappeared. In its place, a desiccated version of civic learning has emerged. In schools, it is often reduced to mere instrumental knowledge like the ability to recite facts about a bicameral legislature or requirements for presidential candidates. Having relegated civics education to the schools, colleges largely erased it from the curriculum and assigned any societal involvement to student affairs.

The last decade or so, however, has seen a growing insistence that a balance be restored between educating for knowledge and educating for democratic citizenship. The call to reclaim or, in some cases, to redefine the civic mission of schools and colleges has come from several locus points. Reports about American disengagement from civic and political life have prompted widespread concern about how such abandonment affects the quality of community life and democratic structures. More disturbing for educators is evidence that the younger the person, the greater the political disengagement and societal disconnection. Such trends do not bode well for assuring the informed, engaged, and empowered citizenry the nation and the globe require in an increasingly complex, interdependent world.

Within the academy, new attention to education's dual societal and scholarly mission has led to a growing move to interconnect scholarship and society in support of education's broader purposes. In the K–12 sector, programs and pedagogy have involved students actively in civic life and community: the Education Commission of the States (2000) has provided particular leadership in this regard.

Since the early 1990s, AAC&U has argued that civic engagement for a diverse democracy must be an integral part of a contemporary liberal education. The American Commitments project, with its report, *The Drama of Diversity and Democracy: Higher Education and American Commitments* (AAC&U 1995), explained diversity as both integral to academic excellence and also a moral barometer of democracy in the United States.

No stable or just democracy can be sustained without building citizens' capacities for living in association across significant cultural difference, and a growing consensus is recognizing education's civic role in this regard. Educational institutions at all levels need to contribute to creating among students a set of dispositions and skills to enhance citizenship, foster a sense of connectedness to a diverse community beyond the classroom, and ultimately, support the practices, basic values, and institutions necessary for democratic processes.

Overlapping Outcomes

Complex learning fits poorly into arbitrary boxes, and so it will be evident that the four outcomes examined by the forum groups will often overlap. A curricular or instructional focus on one of them can easily foster another. Intentional planning to use classroom methods and curricular design to advance simultaneously several outcomes is not only possible but desirable and fruitful.

A quick review of the outcomes as defined reveals similarities that suggest instructional or curricular efficiencies. All four outcomes

- require critical questioning;
- draw upon multiple resources or perspectives to guide thinking and action;
- can involve complex problem solving and application to "real-world" issues;
- require acknowledging, grappling with, and probing into differences (be they in disciplines, cultures, social groups, research results, etc.).

Thus, *inquiry* into the local consequences of importing goods and services from around the *globe* could have students *integrating* readings in history, geography, and economics, as well as information gained from *engagement with local community groups*. This idea of overlapping outcomes, combined with multifunctional teaching and learning practices, is illustrated in chapter 5.

The four outcomes selected for attention by the forum, while drawn from the Greater Expectations concept of an intentional learner, have been identified as important by many stakeholder groups:

- Business leaders cite the importance of integrative learning, analytical thinking, ability to work in diverse teams, and knowledge of the world (AAC&U 2005a; Business–Higher Education Forum 1999).
- State standards for learning in primary and secondary schools call for students to integrate learning, think critically, appreciate diversity, and become responsible citizens in the American democracy.[4]

---

[4]For examples, see New York State's learning standards (www.emsc.nysed.gov) or the Vermont Framework of Standards and Learning Opportunities (www.state.vt.us/educ/new/html/pubs/framework.html), both accessed 11/19/05.

- Standards from the disciplinary associations uniformly include one, two, or more of the outcomes, sometimes at all grade levels from kindergarten through college graduation (e.g., National Council of Teachers of Mathematics 2000).
- Accreditors, both specialized and regional, have reached consensus in support of all four outcomes (among others) as important general outcomes of the baccalaureate degree (AAC&U 2004).
- Regulations from the U.S. Department of Education and legislation from Congress support the outcomes as important learning for all students (U.S. Department of Education 1998).

Despite widespread agreement on the need to foster achievement of the four learning outcomes, the organization of educational institutions erects barriers and sends misleading messages to both students and teachers about knowledge and the kinds of learning that are most important. All too often, institutional and curricular structures suggest that

- the most useful knowledge and skills can be compartmentalized into courses or disciplines;
- the most important problems can be solved from the perspective of a single discipline or method;
- education is really about accumulating rather than constructing knowledge;
- the mastery of a single discipline is the ultimate goal of college education;
- learning is most likely to occur when "experts" impart to students their knowledge;
- learning occurs only in classrooms.

Each of these assumptions undermines efforts to advance the sophisticated, cross-cutting learning represented by the four outcomes. The programs and practices discussed in this monograph all communicate a different understanding of teaching, learning, and institutional intention. What became abundantly clear through the forum's regional seminars was the importance of both initial and ongoing administrative support for programs that intentionally foster liberal learning. While intentionality implies dedicated planning and teaching, its achievement depends upon institutional commitment to a supportive, learning-centered environment. ■

CHAPTER 4

Powerful Curricular and Pedagogic Practices

*T*HE REGIONAL SEMINARS ORGANIZED BY THE FORUM WORKING GROUPS surfaced exciting examples of innovative teaching and learning, at both the individual course and the programmatic levels. While such courses and programs exemplified quite varied designs, to facilitate student learning in the four outcomes, they used a surprisingly small number of curricular and pedagogical practices:

- learning communities
- first-year experiences
- senior capstones or culminating experiences
- service learning
- experiential learning
- authentic tasks, such as collaborative projects, student research, and creative projects
- problem-based learning
- interdisciplinary instruction

Effective Curricular and Pedagogical Practices

Learning communities

Learning communities are curricular architectural elements that enroll a cohort of students in an institutionally designated cluster of at least two linked courses during a given term (or longer). They tend to address academic and social development inside and outside the classroom through planned interactions among the students and teaching faculty. Learning community models range from the simple pairing of two courses to the tight linking of three or four courses with an integrative seminar. Many colleges and universities use some type of learning community in the first year or as part of general education because it builds a sense of belonging and fosters explicit connections. Barbara Leigh Smith, former codirector of the National Learning Communities project at the Evergreen State College, suggests that there are currently some 650 colleges and universities offering some form of learning communities (private communication, January 2006).

Research on learning communities suggests that they result in higher levels of student academic achievement as measured by grade point averages, critical thinking skills, and retention rates (Tinto, Love, and Russo 1994); improve students' intellectual development (Avens and Zelley 1992); and have a positive impact on students' adjustment to college life (Brower 1997). Participants in learning communities also report greater interaction with their peers and more involvement in campus activities (Johnson and King 1997).

First-year experiences

First-year experiences include curricular and/or cocurricular programs beyond orientation that bring together faculty members and groups of first-year students. They tend to address the development of skills, information, and/or perspectives for college success; promote meaningful student–faculty interaction (one-on-one or in small groups); and develop intellectual or living groups through activities, teamwork, and shared goals. First-year experiences can be heavily content based or have a stronger emphasis on adapting to college-level study. They may include intensive writing practice or be part of a multiyear interdisciplinary core program. No matter the exact design, first-year experiences set entering students on their trajectory through college and so can provide an anchor to a purposeful pathway.

Senior capstones or culminating experiences

Senior capstones or culminating experiences are credit-bearing, integrative experiences offered in the last stages of a student's program of studies. In the best cases, they encourage synthesis of the whole academic experience, often through the creation of a product that demonstrates an ability to frame and resolve an open-ended question. While frequently a requirement in a departmental major, capstones can also be tied to general education or even bridge disciplinary and more general learning. Like first-year experiences, they can profitably provide a touch-point on a purposeful pathway and serve as a locus for assessing student learning over time and across courses.

Service learning

Service learning involves students in community-based educational experiences and other service-related activities. In collaboration with the leadership institutions in its Greater Expectations initiative, AAC&U defined service-learning as a credit-bearing instructional strategy that provides students with both meaningful service opportunities in interactive partnership with the community and academic structures for analysis of their contributions and learning. Jacoby (1996, 5) emphasizes "experiential education in which students engage in activities that address human and community needs together with structured opportunities intentionally designed to promote student learning and development." Oates and Leavitt (2003, 7) have noted further that service learning's "philosophy is rooted in cognitive learning research, in which meaning is created out of a concern for social, cultural, or environmental needs."

Research shows that by integrating field experiences into credit-bearing courses and providing opportunities for students to reflect on their community contributions, an institution can enhance the effectiveness of service-learning programs (Astin et al. 2000). In recent years, interest in service learning has exploded in both the K–12 and higher education sectors. While clearly a strategy to advance civic learning, service learning also has been employed to foster inquiry, integrative learning, and global learning.

Experiential learning

Experiential learning includes internships, cooperative education, and field placements (and also service learning); in other words, programs that actively involve students in practical work outside the campus environment. They allow for the practical application of classroom learning in a real-world setting. Many experiential learning opportunities are preplanned by students with advisers or faculty members, carry academic credit or other recognition, require structured reflection and/or an end product, and involve supervision and evaluation (by a professor, field supervisor, or cooperating professional directing the learning activity).

"Authentic" tasks, such as collaborative projects, student research, and creative projects

Authentic tasks mimic the work of practitioners. In collaborative projects, groups of students work together to complete assignments, solve problems, or create products or performances. The active, social nature of collaborative learning—with group members talking, sharing ideas, and making decisions—contrasts with the typical lecture format in which the teacher professes and students passively listen. In grappling with unscripted, complex problems or challenging issues, groups gather, process, and synthesize information while moving toward a resolution. Research points toward motivational, social, and cognitive benefits from collaboration (Johnson, Johnson, and Smith 1991). Employers frequently cite the ability to work in teams as an important skill for new hires.

Cooperative learning is a special kind of collaborative learning in which each group member receives a specific assignment through which he or she contributes to the team effort. Success depends upon all group members working first independently and then collectively.

Student research or creative projects involve self-directed academic work carried out by an individual or by a small group. The topic often addresses open-ended issues or situations; a substantial scholarly or creative product that can be formally presented is usually expected as a culmination of the effort. Such student research or creative endeavor is guided by a faculty mentor with students understanding and acting in their roles as researchers/creators. Student research is a well-documented teaching and learning practice to advance inquiry and integration, requiring by its very nature a range of knowledge, skills, and interactions. While in the past colleges and universities may have required honors students and seniors to produce research papers, today institutions have begun to encourage student participation in research projects throughout the undergraduate years. An increasing number of high school students, too, are involved in research through summer programs sponsored by colleges, universities, and businesses. At both the college and high school levels, sophisticated faculty-led research projects may include students as part of a collaborative research team.

Problem-based learning

Problem-based learning can refer both to a teaching strategy that asks students to solve problems and to a more formal technique abbreviated as PBL. The latter developed first in medical education and, while most often found in the sciences and science-based professions, has also been adapted to the humanities and social sciences. It is a collaborative teaching/learning strategy that employs specific parameters: small working groups of students presented with professional, public, or personal problems they would likely encounter in real life. The team determines the information needed to deal with the problem, gathers that information, and reports out the findings; the process is then repeated until the answer satisfies the team. PBL asks students to assume responsibility for their learning as they conduct research to formulate a thesis rather than simply write about a topic. Both problem solving and PBL function well with elementary and highly complex issues.

Interdisciplinary instruction[5]

Instruction that draws on multiple disciplines mirrors the changes that have occurred in scholarly fields and in the approaches to solving the world's complex natural scientific and social problems. Particularly in the sciences but in other domains as well, breakthroughs have tended to occur where traditional disciplinary areas intersect (whether in astrophysics, molecular biology, or digital photography).

As Klein notes, interdisciplinary programs are not a new phenomenon in U.S. colleges and universities. "In the 1940s, American studies and area studies emerged. In the 1960s and 1970s, women's studies, environmental studies, and urban studies entered the academy. . . . Since 1945, many new fields have been hybrid in nature, and in the closing decade of the [twentieth] century, interdisciplinary fields [were] greater in number and visibility" (Klein 1999, 7). Klein notes further that many large and even mid-sized institutions offer a range of interdisciplinary fields and majors (including gerontology, criminology, policy studies, material sciences, legal studies, and peace studies). Possibly because they are less bounded by traditions, these interdisciplinary programs tend to be fertile incubation sites for innovations in teaching and learning. At the secondary school level, too, interdisciplinary instruction increasingly characterizes creative high schools.

*   *   *

When well planned and conducted, the curricular and pedagogic practices described above have great potential to develop the four outcomes of interest and, by extension, intentional learners. They often ask students to attempt to solve complex, real-world problems by engaging in analysis, synthesis, and evaluation as information is gathered and then solutions are proposed and critiqued. Such active involvement of students in their learning tends to move them toward the top levels of the cognitive domain (from

---

[5]This publication will not delve into the fray of distinguishing among interdisciplinarity, multidisciplinarity, and cross-disciplinarity.

application up through evaluation) while traditional lecture-based classes focus more on the lower levels of knowledge and comprehension. Gardiner (1994, 50) points out that the traditional practice of delivering facts through lectures retards the already slow process of student intellectual and moral development.

Additional learning activities featured at the regional seminars, often embedded within the practices above, include (1) reflective writing and speaking and/or reflective seminars, and (2) student self-assessment.

Reflective journals and essays are valuable tools for deepening the comprehension initiated through service learning and other educational experiences. Reflection need not be a shallow rehashing of emotions and events. Rather it can direct students, through explicit goals or a series of questions, to think in detail about the integration of course content with out-of-class experiences, or theory with practice. Students can examine personal values, attitudes, and knowledge, and then reconcile those reflections with new values, attitudes, and knowledge. Researchers have found that reflection results in the formation of new concepts and generalizations that the learner then tests through additional experiences. Such learning tends to be well retained. Teachers can assess reflective writing based upon the quality of student responses to guiding questions or goals that structure the reflective experience.

Self-assessment asks students to bring an objective analysis to their accomplishments. For each assignment, descriptions of expectations (standards), grading scales, and examples of performance at the unacceptable, acceptable, and superior levels (rubrics) help bring rigor to the self-assessment exercise. Involving students in evaluating their own work validates them as active participants in the teaching–learning process.

Both reflection and self-assessment engage students in metacognition, i.e., thinking about their own learning. Such thinking produces insights for students and teachers alike about how well concepts are understood and which topics require further clarification. Metacognition empowers students to take responsibility for their own learning over time, contributing significantly to their development as intentional learners. Bereiter and Scardamalia (1989) explain how metacognition includes self-regulation, which involves the ability to orchestrate one's learning (to plan, monitor success, and correct errors when appropriate—all necessary for effective intentional learning). The "integration of meta-cognitive instruction with discipline-based learning can enhance student achievement and develop in students the ability to learn independently" (Bransford, Brown, and Cocking 2000, 21). Teaching practices congruent with a metacognitive approach to learning—those that focus on making meaning, self-assessment, and reflection about what did and did not work—have been shown to increase the degree to which students transfer their learning to new settings and events (summarized by Bransford, Brown, and Cocking 2000; see p. 12 for original sources).

Using the Instructional Practices More Intentionally

Intentionality remains a central issue in facilitating student learning, regardless of the practices selected. Simply adopting a particular curricular design or employing an instructional method does not assure the desired learning outcomes. For example,

- assigning a cohort of students to the same sections of two courses may conform to the definition of a learning community, but without coordinated reflective seminars, a conscious echoing of themes, or well-chosen authentic assignments students may miss the connections and opportunities to integrate across the curriculum;
- the various disciplinary perspectives that enrich interdisciplinary study can remain invisible to students without faculty guidance on understanding their differences;
- independent or collaborative research can develop inquiry capacities, but the learning will be deepened if the students are asked to justify their selection of questions and methods.

The group of eight commonly used practices offers good potential for fostering achievement in the four outcomes and for developing intentional learners; creative faculty members have used them successfully to do so. However, maximizing this potential—by actively engaging students in their learning, and designing-in self-assessment and reflection—can enhance both actual achievement and institutional intentionality.

The following chart maps the eight educational practices against the four selected learning outcomes both in terms of current use and future potential. It is based upon observations from the regional seminars and from campus visits by the authors and other AAC&U staff members.

Powerful Educational Practices and the Four Learning Outcomes

	Learning communities	First-year experiences	Senior capstones or culminating experiences	Service learning	Experiential learning	"Authentic" tasks, such as collaborative projects, student research, and creative projects	Problem-based learning	Interdisciplinary instruction
Integrative learning	F	F	F	F	F	F	F	F
Inquiry learning	F	F	F	F	F	F	F	F
Global learning	L	L	L	F	F	L	L	F
Civic learning	L	F	L	F	F	L	L	F

F = frequently used to facilitate an outcome
L = less commonly used to facilitate an outcome but with good potential

An institution desiring to enhance overall intentionality in instruction will want to explore changes in both pedagogy and curricular design to foster improvement in student learning. Local institutional politics, resources, leadership, and culture will influence the degree to which the focus is on the curriculum, on teaching practices, or on a combination. Neither an elegant curricular design nor an engaging pedagogy alone will be effective without a supportive climate, careful alignment of goals and methods, and authentic assessments for improvement.

Attention to the following principles can help improve purposeful achievement of the important outcomes of a practical and engaged liberal education:

- Select instructional practices that align with and have good potential to advance the desired outcomes.
- Maximize the potential of the chosen practice to make it an effective and efficient learning experience.
- Assure that students are *doing* what they are supposed to be learning—that their experiences mirror the real work of an expert in the field.
- Require periodic reflection and self-assessment to deepen analysis, synthesis, evaluation, and integration.
- Set clear and high learning expectations for all students. Choose a combination of course-level, curricular, and programmatic strategies to achieve the desired level of achievement.

The importance of clearly stated outcomes cannot be overemphasized. Outcomes set the direction of learning, ideally they guide decisions about curricular design and pedagogy, and they delimit the elements of achievement monitored through assessment (refer to the Cycle of Intentional Learning on p. 4). In *The Art and Science of Assessing General Education Outcomes* (2005), Leskes and Wright discuss converting broad outcomes into specific and assessable objectives. ■

CHAPTER 5

Creating Purposeful Pathways

THE CURRICULAR AND PEDAGOGICAL ELEMENTS DESCRIBED IN CHAPTER 4 CAN PROVIDE THE BUILDING BLOCKS OF PURPOSEFUL SEQUENCES OF LEARNING. Their use in developmental and carefully sequenced ways—from high school through college—could maximize achievement for all students. While no true examples of such cross-sector pathways surfaced during the forum's work, many individual elements did, and these were used in interesting and potentially powerful ways.

This chapter presents three different kinds of purposeful pathways: hypothetical pathways constructed from actual practices selected from several institutions, descriptions of individual institutional programs that advance multiple outcomes, and single-institution efforts advancing one particular outcome.

The hypothetical pathways were constructed by the authors to illustrate how an outcome might be developed beginning in high school and advanced through first-year, middle, and capstone experiences at the college level. The charts on pages 36–39 indicate how to make expectations transparent to students and reinforce learning of the intended outcome through aligned pedagogical choices.

The stories from individual campuses on pages 41–45 were selected as examples of programs where intentional instructional choices resulted in the efficient and effective co-development of several outcomes. Given the difficulty of finding the time needed to advance the learning now expected of students, such efficiencies are highly desirable.

The charts that close the chapter include short descriptions of approaches to developing the four outcomes from selected high schools, community colleges, four-year campuses, and national projects. These approaches came to the attention of the working groups and the authors primarily during the regional "reflective seminars," but also as a result of periodic campus visits and discussions with colleagues.

The examples are presented to the reader not with the intent that a practice simply be adopted, but to help trigger imaginative adaptation to local circumstances, student characteristics, resources, and institutional mission. The stories, while short, are meant to provide "food for thought" by revealing diverse, creative ways in which educators shape programs to lead students to achieve sophisticated outcomes and meet expectations for learning and doing.

A Purposeful Pathway for Integrative Learning

Curricular strategy	Transparency	Classroom practices	Example
Step 1. In high school, students study across two disciplines such as literature and history.	The teacher makes clear to the students the expectation that they will gain experience, at a novice level, in using knowledge from multiple disciplines as they analyze and think about issues.	Assignments and classroom discussion prompt students to draw from each discipline as they probe an issue in depth.	*New Britain High School, Connecticut* In an American studies course integrating American history and literature, students read *The Crucible* and *The Scarlet Letter*, visit a museum of colonial art, and read extracts from primary and secondary historical sources. Integration is fostered through discussion of Puritan beliefs, the larger historical timeframe, and the play and novel. Teachers provide literary and historical clues as students struggle to answer significant questions in both disciplines.
Step 2. First-year students enroll in a two-semester-long experience that pairs courses around a theme or a challenging social issue.	The expectation that students will learn to draw on knowledge from several domains to understand, synthesize, and examine their own beliefs is repeatedly stated. If writing improvement is part of the sequence, the importance of communication is stressed.	The close textual reading, analytical writing, and intellectual discourse that will prepare students for more advanced study can be combined with analysis from multiple perspectives. A topic introduced in the first course can be more deeply examined in the second. Written assignments can ask students to seek knowledge from various sources to build a convincing case. Guided reflection on the process of integration can further deepen learning.	*Bard College* All first-year students have a common academic experience starting with the three-week Language and Thinking Workshop in August that requires both intensive discussion and writing. A two semester first-year seminar (current theme: What is Enlightenment? The Science, Culture, and Politics of Reason) is centered on a core group of texts as well as weekly symposia that include visiting speakers, panels, debates, and concerts. Substantial analytical writing in both semesters and discussions in the symposia engage students in addressing diverse ideas in an articulate way.
Step 3. In the foundational, intermediate, or advanced courses in the majors (including the professions) students undertake experiential learning related to their fields of study.	The links between theoretical learning and application and the value of those linkages in specific disciplines are carefully explained by professors.	Students are asked to use their developing expertise in new situations and put theory into practice through case study analysis, projects, field work, internships, or cooperative education.	*Babson College* Business students choose an idea for a business, develop a marketing plan, and run the business for a specified length of time while enrolled in courses that deliver "just in time" information for the process.
Step 4. In the senior year, students complete a required capstone (in the major, general education, or a combination) that reviews, further develops, and assesses knowledge, skills, attitudes, and perspectives acquired over an entire education: in general education, the major, experiential learning, and the cocurriculum.	In explaining the capstone requirement, the department and individual professors stress the expectation for integration within the discipline, as well as across disciplines and life experiences.	A comprehensive research paper, team project, internship, or seminar prompts students to draw upon all aspects of their learning and knowledge from at least two disciplines to demonstrate advanced levels of synthesis, analysis, evaluation, and/or performance/creative work.	*Yale University* A theater major directs a production of *Hamlet*, using knowledge of directing techniques and of the play and familiarity with the Elizabethan era. In an accompanying analytical paper, the student explains how his or her interpretation relates to theater history/theory, professional productions, and to a close textual reading. He or she may also utilize a feminist or psychosocial analysis to explain directing and acting choices.

A Purposeful Pathway for Inquiry Learning

Curricular strategy	Transparency	Classroom practices	Example
Step 1. In high school, students enroll in a theme-based academy of three or four linked courses that promote synthesis through projects.	Advisers and teachers stress the goals of answering questions and justifying the answers, framing new questions, and relating raw data to the questions.	Teachers provide guiding questions, prompts, models, frameworks, and suggested sites for information. They use direct observation, case studies, simulations, and role playing.	*Sir Francis Drake High School in San Anselmo, California* Students study the election process by creating video campaign ads for candidates or issues in an upcoming election. They also make "process" Web sites that lead them to reflect upon their learning and thinking.
Step 2. First-year seminars and selected courses in general education introduce learning through specific problems/projects/ assignments.	Professors make explicit the outcomes of further developing powers of observation, synthesis, and problem posing as well as expectations in reflection and analysis. Critical thinking is stressed as a goal of the first-year seminars/courses and of the entire institution.	Writing assignments and/or oral presentations ask students to identify a problem/issue and devise ways to resolve it. Professors provide guidelines and format. Techniques might include journals, brainstorming, teamwork, or demonstrations.	*Indiana University–Purdue University Indianapolis* A first-year learning community for students in engineering includes an investigation of reverse engineering, instruction on creating a Web page, an introduction to engineering careers, and a look at professional organizations. It also includes a group research paper, teamwork topics, and a PowerPoint presentation.
Step 3. Problem-based learning occurs in disciplinary courses as students begin their majors.	Professors discuss critical observation, problem posing and problem solving, synthesis, analysis, and interpretation of complex issues in the discipline. At the institutional level, facilities support problem-based learning and inquiry is stressed as an institutional priority for all majors.	Projects based on complex issues/problems of the field ask students to draw on their specific content knowledge as well as on their developing powers of synthesis, analysis, and interpretation. Students pose their own questions and devise ways of answering them. Active, hands-on learning could alternate with lectures that provide "just-in-time" information that students can apply immediately.	*Samford University* A junior-year, foundational nursing course includes a problem-based-learning model for each key concept. Progressing through the course involves advancing from simple to complex concepts. A module, which might last from several days to one month, could focus, for example, on nursing a child with fatigue brought about by sickle cell anemia. Students form groups early in the course to work through the problems posed.
Step 4. At the senior level, a capstone project or thesis in the major (or in general education) culminates the inquiry approach to learning by asking students to draw on the knowledge and skills acquired in the major, general education, electives, and cocurricular experiences.	Course catalogs and departmental information about the senior capstone experience clearly state that the capstone requires advanced critical observa- tion, recording, synthesis, conceptualization, interpretation, and evaluation. Formative assessments during the experience provide reminders of the need for insightful use of data, logic, and diverse resources.	Under faculty guidance, students or teams choose a significant problem/project to research/carry out over a semester or two. The professor could provide guiding questions but the emphasis is on student initiative. The work could be made public through publishing an article or presenting it to community and industry experts.	*Southern Illinois University, Edwardsville* All seniors must complete a capstone that, for computer science majors, consists of a team project that spans two semesters. Ideas for real programming needs are solicited from the university and local community. Students are responsible for all aspects, from establishing initial requirements to implementation and deployment; they need to figure out how to interact with and design products for non-specialist users.

A Purposeful Pathway for Global Learning

Curricular strategy	Transparency	Classroom practices	Example
Step 1. A high school honors course in world history introduces different cultures and worldviews.	Clear knowledge and skill outcomes explain to students what they will learn and be able to do; for example, to see global patterns over time, connect local to global developments, compare societies, put culturally diverse values in historical contexts, and gather evidence.	Students read extracts from primary texts and documents while learning about the geography of the countries studied. They view documentary films, visit museums or Internet sites, and participate in a model UN.	*Advanced Placement World History* Students in AP world history courses learn to examine and use groups of documents as evidence to support an essay about interactions among major societies. Students also learn to suggest other documents that would deepen understanding. The AP exam also requires students to complete this kind of analysis.
Step 2. First-year college courses include collaboration with students in other countries/cultures to work on a project with global and/or cross-cultural dimensions.	The goals specific to the international or cross-cultural collaboration should be both described prior to student enrollment and reinforced throughout the experience. Some of these goals include communicating across cultures, working in diverse teams, and understanding the perspectives of others.	Professors could use e-mail, chat rooms, joint Web sites, video conferencing, and study abroad trips that engage international groups of students from the various countries. The issue or problem could be suggested by businesses, governments, or NGO partners. Formative assessments and self-reflection through journals monitor the success of each student in the cross-cultural collaborative relationships.	*Pennsylvania State University* An introduction to engineering design course has teams of students from France and the United States work to improve the system of springs and gears by which a pop-up camper trailer roof is lifted.
Step 3. A campus center for international studies sponsors activities for students at all class levels, and provides support and opportunities for advancing oral language skills and study of a particular region of the world. Summer internships abroad supplement on-campus learning.	Advisers make public and reinforce clear program goals: to experience first-hand a culture other than one's own, to see one's own culture from the perspective of others, and to communicate on a daily basis in a foreign language.	Courses in language study concentrate on conversational and professional language usage to ensure cultural competence of learners. Study abroad is rigorously prepared for and debriefed. A tangible outcome from an internship (e.g., an article, a project, or a Web site) could provide direct evidence of student achievement.	*Connecticut College* The Center for International Study and the Liberal Arts supports a program in which students are funded to spend a summer internship in the country on which they are focusing their studies.
Step 4. A senior capstone asks students to bring global perspectives or international issues into a research or experiential project in the major.	The institution emphasizes its expectations in global learning for all students, no matter their majors (e.g., the ability to place one's work in a cross-cultural or global perspective or the ability to see global implications of one's field). These outcomes would be emphasized in general education and in the major programs.	Students might be asked to submit a research paper written in a foreign language or one that uses sources from other cultures/languages; to present in a foreign language or from the perspective of another culture; or to analyze an issue in the major field drawing on cross-cultural comparisons.	*Connecticut College, continued* As a follow-up to the summer internship, students complete a senior seminar and integrative project that explores issues related to the major, the international arena, and the foreign language/culture studied and experienced.

A Purposeful Pathway for Civic Learning

Curricular strategy	Transparency	Classroom practices	Example
Step 1. During high school, drawing on the experience of democracy in students' own communities and cultures, the class explores a public issue of common concern and completes a project based on a genuine community need.	The intentions of the course—to learn about one's own culture and government, to hone observational skills, to understand how individual and collective efforts can help solve community problems—are reinforced through clear outcomes and detailed project assignments. The entire school community commits to the course outcomes. Public presentations of completed community projects showcase the process and results.	Students role play, find newspaper articles, interview family members and relevant citizens, and complete team projects, including service learning, in community settings.	*CityWorks program of the Constitutional Rights Foundation, Los Angeles* The program infuses interactive lessons on local government into mainstream government or civics courses. CityWorks involves groups of students in researching community problems, examining relevant policies, planning and implementing action, and then documenting and evaluating their experiences.
Step 2. Freshmen enroll in an intentionally diverse living/learning community that includes service learning and facilitates the transition to college, especially for first-generation students.	Discussions reinforce the intended personal, identity development, and civic outcomes of the program. Admissions and program staff members recruit students to the program using testimonials and multimedia presentations. Academic and personal support services are embedded in the residential project.	Primary and secondary sources introduce concepts of inequality, struggles for democracy and inclusion, the self, and the other. Debates, reflective journals, and oral presentations help students deepen the learning from their service activities.	*University of Michigan Community Scholars Program* In this residential learning community, students, faculty, and community partners pursue critical analysis of community issues, meaningful service learning, intercultural understanding, and dialogue. Some students from past classes return to serve as peer leaders and advisers.
Step 3. An intermediate course in the major involves students learning about or bringing their developing disciplinary competency to bear on a local community problem.	Admissions materials and departmental descriptions during enrollment and advising convey a clear institutional commitment to civic engagement. Civic engagement outcomes and the means to achieve them are presented clearly in syllabi for courses.	Issues of interest to the local, regional, national, or global society form the context in which disciplinary learning occurs. Through analysis of data, community art projects, or local economic development trends, students see the direct links between their classroom studies and the needs of the larger society.	*Trinity College (Connecticut)* Students in a sociology course transform raw police data into a form usable by the local neighborhood planning group. Another course on urban architecture focuses on cities and their inhabitants.
Step 4. Senior capstone service-learning projects—completed in collaborative, multidisciplinary teams—draw upon learning in both general education and the major area.	In explaining graduation requirements, the university is extremely careful to include prerequisites, the process, and outcomes of the senior capstone in service learning. Cooperation between community agencies and the campus placement office ensures excellent communication of goals for each placement, responsibilities of student teams, and lines of authority for supervision and assessment.	Using student teams to develop sophisticated solutions to authentic and difficult problems confronting community agencies demands high levels of personal responsibility and the ability to collaborate across multiple differences. Students engage in improving people's lives.	*Portland State University* The senior capstone features collaborative learning communities of students from different majors working on community projects. The six-credit course provides an integrative, culminating experience in social engagement and intercultural cooperative problem solving in the urban campus's local community.

Examples of Educational Practices to Advance the Four Outcomes

Dozens of institutions and hundreds of practitioners described their work at the forum's reflective seminars. Many more are working assiduously to advance important liberal learning outcomes. The examples selected for inclusion in this section represent a variety of levels, institutions, approaches, and practices. They come from high schools, community colleges, four-year colleges, and universities. Some regional or national programs have been adopted by several schools.

It should be no surprise that students can make progress in each of the four outcomes during high school. They do not arrive in college fully unformed. Ideally, meaningful sequences of learning would begin at the primary and secondary levels to provide a foundation for traditional-age students. Keys to success for a high school to college pathway include identification of the key knowledge and skills needed for successful college entry; improvements in teaching and learning both in high school and in college; and alignment of expectations and learning practices.

As already explained, the four outcomes do not divide cleanly one from another. *Civic learning* can—and most likely will—involve *integrating* experiences from the classroom with those from community work. Interdisciplinary, *integrative* study may occur in the context of *global* learning. Campuses that have most effectively put into place programs to advance the outcomes intentionally end up advancing several at the same time. They have devised efficient and effective structures that embody the concept of multifunctionality: their programs accomplish many things at the same time. This section begins with descriptions of five such efficient and innovative campuses that also have designed their programs into purposeful pathways; it concludes with additional examples of institutions and organizations that have created exemplary programs, curricula, courses, or activities to advance at least one of the four learning outcomes. While several institutions were recommended to the authors as good examples in more than one outcome (for example, the University of Delaware for inquiry through an institutional emphasis in problem-based learning and for a curricular pathway in global learning), we generally included only one such example, choosing to cite additional campuses where possible.

Worcester Polytechnic Institute (WPI)

Integration through inquiry-based projects, civic learning, and global learning

At WPI, most students major in science, engineering, or management. More than thirty years ago, the institute changed its graduation requirements from prescribed sets of courses to a sequence of three projects through which students both advance and demonstrate their learning. The projects all are based on inquiry, each with a different integrative emphasis.

- *Integration of humanities or arts:* All lower-division students complete a three-credit-hour project on a theme they identify as running through at least five previous courses. Usually completed in the sophomore year, this project most often takes the form of an original research paper or creative work. The intent is to provide students with sufficient familiarity in an area of the humanities or arts to promote a lifelong interest.

- *Integration of science/technology with societal concerns:* Intermediate-level students (mostly juniors) complete a nine-credit-hour interdisciplinary, practical project at the interface of science/technology and society. The intent of this civic learning is for all students to understand, as professionals and as citizens, how science and technology both affect and are shaped by social structures. Sixty percent of projects occur at WPI's centers around the world, where teams of students solve such problems as soil pollution abatement in Thailand, sewage disposal in Venice, or botanical garden design in Costa Rica. All projects terminate with a technical report and oral presentation to a faculty committee.

- *Integration within the major field and of theory with practice:* All seniors complete a nine-credit-hour project in their major at a level appropriate to a beginning graduate student or an entry-level professional. The intent is for students to demonstrate that they can apply the appropriate facts, theories, methodologies, and analytic skills of their major area to frame and solve a problem. Depending on the discipline, the focus may be on design, synthesis, experimentation, or theoretical investigation.

Commentary: WPI's sequence of rigorous projects models a purposeful pathway. At least three different kinds of integration are developed through inquiry, culminating in a professional-level outcome. Students move from depth and integration in general studies to depth and integration in major studies. As many students complete one or more of the projects during an international placement, they also develop global learning; WPI has the second highest percentage among doctoral-granting institutions of students with international experience. The program also stresses other important outcomes: effective writing, oral communication, and teamwork. The global component could be further strengthened if it were introduced at the beginning of college and then reinforced in the senior year.

Hampshire College

Integration over time through inquiry, community service, and global learning

At Hampshire College, students qualify for the Bachelor of Arts degree by completing a program composed of three divisions (levels) of study, each of which is based on learning through inquiry. In Division I, taken the first three semesters, students are introduced to inquiry skills by enrolling in a first-year tutorial with their advisers and completing eight courses over the college's five schools, each course stressing inquiry in a domain of knowledge. The third semester is set aside for a systematic evaluation of and reflection on the first-year work, leading to the creation by each student of a plan for Division II in which prior learning is applied to a chosen topic or field. This individually designed program can include courses, independent work, and internships or field studies. In Division III (Advanced Studies), students draw on all their previous work as they undertake a concluding independent project centered on a specific question or idea.

In addition to these requirements, to foster civic learning, students complete service to the college or the surrounding community. In their concluding projects, they are encouraged to look beyond the specific focus of their work and to integrate considerations and experiences of the community at large into their scholarship. The faculty also asks all students to introduce multiple cultural perspectives into their concentrations and projects.

Commentary: One important aspect of the Hampshire College purposeful pathway is the development of students' responsibilities for their learning. As they pursue a topic of interest over time, and integrate material into their projects from many fields and courses, Hampshire students develop the deep understanding that allows learning to transfer from one environment to another. As with WPI, if the global component were stressed at several points it would further reinforce the centrality of global learning.

Wagner College

Integration and civic engagement through learning communities and service learning

At the beginning, middle, and end of their time on campus, Wagner College students participate in courses linked into learning communities. All first-year students enroll in a learning community that includes (a) two carefully articulated courses from different disciplines linked by a common theme, (b) a reflective tutorial to reinforce the common theme while stressing writing and research skills, and (c) thirty hours of fieldwork directly related to the learning community theme. As examples, over the past several years, students have engaged in this service learning at the Bowery Soup Kitchen, Public School Literacy Programs, and New York Urban League.

All students repeat this curricular pattern in either their sophomore or junior year through intermediate learning communities, and then again as seniors where the learning community combines a major course, a reflective tutorial, and an internship. The sequence of learning communities involves progressively more intense and extensive community involvement.

Commentary: Wagner College's purposeful pathways include both general education and the major. Multiple opportunities allow students to integrate across disciplines, between the academy and the local community, and between content-based courses and writing seminars. Civic learning, as a focus of the learning community model, also becomes a mechanism for integration and cumulatively more advanced learning over time.

Portland State University

Integration and inquiry through learning communities, interdisciplinary courses, service learning, and collaborative projects

Students who spend four years at Portland State University experience a general education ladder that advances integration, inquiry, and civic learning. Learning communities, interdisciplinary courses, and service learning—often in combination—serve as the curricular vehicles.

Starting in the freshman year, students enroll in a sequence of team-designed, thematically linked courses that stress the process of inquiry: framing questions, gathering evidence, analyzing the evidence, and communicating the results. Their studies might, for example, involve them in community-based issues such as the control of ivy growth in public parks or citizen use of the downtown area. In the sophomore year, each student selects three term-long inquiry courses that each introduce a conceptual framework for a cross-disciplinary area of study. At the junior/senior level, students take a group of inquiry-based courses from one of the cluster topic areas introduced at the sophomore year. These emphasize the human condition and social responsibility. For example, the three-course European Studies Cluster provides an in-depth study of history, politics, geography, theater, art, and literature to convey the complexity of the past and present European scene. The Drama as Politics course in this cluster stresses the stage as a forum for portraying ethical issues of human experience and for presenting social issues.

Seniors capitalize on this preparation, as well as on an upper-division integrated cluster linked to the sophomore inquiry topic, to engage in capstone work. An interdisciplinary team of seniors undertakes a problem of real concern to the community, using the city as a learning laboratory. The team might help a community agency write grant proposals or conduct needs assessments or it might interview elders for an oral history archive.

All parts of the general education program stress the process of learning and how to find, judge, and use information. Mastery of these skills is assessed through electronic portfolios.

Commentary: Through the students themselves, Portland State's model integrates the major and general education in the senior collaborative project. Each student brings his or her area of concentration expertise to the problem at hand. Such a multi-perspective team, attacking a real-world issue, authentically reproduces life after college thereby extending the purposeful pathway to the world of work. Portland State illustrates how even an urban, comprehensive university can provide exciting, sequential learning of important outcomes.

St. Edward's University

Civic learning, inquiry, and global learning through integration and interdisciplinary study

The general education program at St. Edward's University includes six required courses over the four college years that lead students to engage with issues of identity, relationships, culture, and moral reasoning (all important to developing civic learning, global learning, and responsible learners). The curriculum uses inquiry methods and interdisciplinary approaches to foster the development of cultural understandings. Students progress from a first-year course on the human experience (that includes small group work and writing) to a two-course, interdisciplinary examination of American culture (including the formulation of solutions to problems facing American society). In the junior year the investigation expands to contemporary world issues, supplemented by a study of moral reasoning. The vertical spine of general education culminates in a capstone course that requires students to investigate a controversial issue in society, analyze the different sides of the issue, propose a resolution to it, communicate the results of the investigation both orally and in a major paper, and finally engage in a supportive civic activity. The academic experience is augmented by cocurricular opportunities including cultural immersion experiences to foreign countries, a model United Nations/Organization of American States program, and an international guest professors series coordinated though the university's Kozmetzky Center for Global Finance.

Commentary: With St. Edward's general education design, the earlier courses, in a purposeful manner, lead students to their culminating integrative challenge. Programs in the academic majors that reinforce civic learning, inquiry, integration, and global learning help deepen even further students' knowledge and intellectual skills.

Bonner Foundation Civic Engagement Certificate

Civic learning, inquiry, and integration through interdisciplinary courses, service learning, and experiential learning

Five colleges—Mars Hill College, the College of New Jersey, Washington and Lee University, University of California–Los Angeles, and Portland State University— have been working to create a civic engagement certificate or minor as an academic complement to a comprehensive community service cocurricular program. Supported by the Fund for the Improvement of Postsecondary Education and organized through the Bonner Foundation, the institutions share a common architecture for students' developmental and sequential civic learning.

Each program has six components. The first is a lead-in course, typically offered the first year through freshmen seminars, learning communities, and first-year orientation courses that include an exploration of service and social justice. As part of the intermediate-level learning, students take three additional kinds of courses: one that addresses poverty issues, one that exposes them to international issues through courses or study abroad, and one that includes a significant service-learning component or community-based research experience as part of the student's major or electives.

To acquire the certificate, students must also complete, though not necessarily for credit, a full-time service internship that offers them an opportunity to encounter issues of poverty, cultural diversity, and public policy. Finally, as the culmination of the certificate program, the students engage in an intense and demanding service placement capstone that will integrate academic work and may be part of a senior seminar, an independent study, or a community-based research project.

Commentary: Although the Bonner Foundation had previously established a well-designed cocurricular student leadership and community service developmental model that spanned four years, this civic engagement curricular adaptation is a superb foil for integrating the opportunities across all dimensions in higher education. The Bonner civic learning model, both curricular and cocurricular, distinguishes itself through its clearly articulated values of educating students to participate intentionally as citizens in the democratic process; developing understandings in order to participate successfully in a global society; advocating for fairness and equality while addressing systematic social and environmental issues; establishing capacities for building vibrant communities; engaging dimensions of diversity in public life; and exploring personal beliefs while respecting the spiritual practices of others.

Examples That Foster Integrative Learning

Example	Summary	Description	Commentary
Wellesley High School (Wellesley, Massachusetts)	*An integrative, interdisciplinary senior-year high school course*	Wellesley High School offers a joint English and social studies course called "Humanities." The course fulfills graduation requirements for both disciplines and examines the concept of identity, including the forces that shape it. Units of study include the individual and collective hopes of the American dream; and innocence, activism, and disillusionment as seen through the Vietnam era and its fallout. The yearlong, senior elective asks students to examine, first objectively and then reflectively, the presence of particular norms of identity within a wide range of ethnic backgrounds. Some of the texts used include *The Autobiography of Malcolm X, A People's History of the United States, Bury My Heart at Wounded Knee, Ethnicity and Family History, Angela's Ashes, Hamlet,* and *The Odyssey.*	A majority of four-year colleges now require all undergraduates to take a course that studies diversity, often including issues of racial/ethnic diversity in American history and culture. The integrative exploration of identity that students experience in the Wellesley High School humanities course will prepare them well for more advanced study of similar issues in college.
South Grand Prairie High School (Grand Prairie, Texas)	*Integrative pathways in high school through learning academies*	The diverse students at South Grand Prairie High School can integrate courses with authentic career experiences through learning community "academies" that help them understand why certain courses are required while they also apply knowledge to solve real-world problems. Each academy consists of multiple, planned "pathways"—coherent courses of study that provide the specific academic and career skills needed for entry into a broad cluster of related occupations and for admission to college. One academy focuses on business and computer technology, for example, and another on the creative and performing arts. By occupying a specific area of the school, each academy can create an intimate environment within a large high school. Teachers can work within a single academy and integrate an academic subject (mathematics, for instance) with particular career pathways. Advanced placement courses are also offered within the academies and draw strong interest, possibly because their relationship to the academy's focus is transparent. Students are permitted to change from one academy to another; their non-career-related courses prepare them for college and exceed the state's requirements for high school graduation. In fact, the Texas minimum program of study is actively discouraged, being offered only through a petition process. Administrative support includes extensive teacher development programs, new teacher mentoring, and school/business partnerships. External grants often supply specialized resources for the program.	The teacher-driven career academy initiative was designed to address the apathy and alienation of the vast "middle majority" of students. With the new academies, learning becomes more relevant as students apply knowledge from academic classes to career-related experiences. The career academy approach has produced higher student achievement, improved attitudes toward school, and built strong connections to the community. The model illustrates successful use of active pedagogy, integration through application, problem solving, and higher expectations for all students.
Project Lead the Way	*Integrative problem-based learning that leads from high school to college*	Interest in problem-based learning has generated projects bridging higher and secondary education and the private sector. Project Lead the Way is one such multi-sector effort that helps high schools to organize a five-course, pre-engineering curriculum that prepares students to enroll and succeed in college science and engineering programs. A school might develop a course such as Introduction to Engineering Design that challenges students to solve design problems while incorporating realistic restraints ranging from environmental law to child safety. A curriculum might easily integrate concepts from science, mathematics, technology, history, geography, and art.	Schools that participate in Project Lead the Way are supported by a strong national organization that serves as a resource for curricular information and models of successful implementation. Sharing experiences helps create innovative curricula without needing to "reinvent the wheel." With a clear goal of leading students from high school to college study, Project Lead the Way models a purposeful pathway that crosses the secondary school–college divide.

Examples That Foster Integrative Learning (cont.)

Example	Summary	Description	Commentary
LaGuardia Community College–City University of New York	*First-year, theme-based learning communities in a community college*	LaGuardia Community College has a variety of learning-community programs organized around themes. Because students originate from more than 140 different countries, the college uses these learning communities to pay special attention to issues of student success. Entering liberal arts and sciences majors can choose from a menu of six to eight themed "clusters" that represent a complete semester's schedule. Each has two courses from the core liberal arts and sciences curriculum plus English composition, a research paper course, and an integrated team-taught hour. Topics for the research paper course are interdisciplinary and draw on all the other courses in the cluster. Another learning community program, the New Student House, offers support for first-year developmental and ESL students through a cluster that connects Basic Reading, Basic Writing, or ESL to a college-level content course and a freshman seminar. In addition, fully half of LaGuardia's ESL courses are integrated with college-level content courses throughout the curriculum. LaGuardia also offers freshman interest groups, which consist of two basic skills courses, a freshman seminar, a college-level course, and a non-credit integrative hour. Both faculty and students in each learning community cohort contribute topics and issues to the integrative seminar.	New Student House participants have a 95 percent first-year retention rate, compared to only 25 percent for students taking a stand-alone version of Basic Skills. Students in the freshmen interest groups also show improved retention. By crafting programs that recognize both student deficiencies on entering college and potential to progress with college-level learning in a discipline, LaGuardia has risen to the challenge of enrolling many students who require developmental study, especially in English and reading. The astounding retention statistic for the New Student House program is an impressive model for achieving greater expectations. The consistent use of reflective seminars builds student habits of metacognition, with its attendant advantages for future learning.
The Evergreen State College	*A comprehensive, inquiry-based approach to integrative learning*	At the Evergreen State College, all instruction is offered through interdisciplinary, multi-professor classes, many of which utilize problem-based learning. A recent catalog included courses such as Environment, Health, and Community; Fishes, Frogs, and Forests; and Sovereignty: Reclaiming Voice and Authority, all of which require students to struggle with creating solutions to real-world problems utilizing multidisciplinary perspectives. Founded as a unique public liberal arts institution, Evergreen has always focused on instructional principles that include active learning, integration of theory and practice, and working with issues and problems found within students' own communities. Professors' narrative assessments of student learning provide rich feedback to students to allow for improved learning as they move through each semester and their chosen degree programs.	While few colleges could fully adopt the Evergreen approach to integrated study, their model of multidisciplinary planning, community involvement, and narrative assessment shows that it is possible to implement a distinctive educational philosophy and sustain innovative practices over time. Evergreen embodies ideas of integration at all levels of instructional planning and can offer much to campuses interested both in how integrative programs can function and what they can teach.
Metropolitan College of New York	*A comprehensive approach to integrating theory and practice*	Students at Metropolitan, most of whom work full time, complete a highly structured "purpose-centered education" that integrates the theory and knowledge gained from the liberal arts with practice in the workplace. Degree programs have eight "purposes" (e.g., in the business program, becoming an effective supervisor or managing change), each of which serves as the integrative focus for one semester. A "purpose" seminar horizontally facilitates integration of all of the semester's knowledge and skills; it consists of a three-hour weekly workshop in which students strive to solve a problem in their workplace or community related to the semester's purpose. Assessment includes teacher-designed course evaluations and "constructive action documents," which are records of the projects completed during the purpose seminars. Scoring procedures for complex assessments are often developed collaboratively by the faculty and revised as needed. Field supervisors, oriented and trained by the faculty, provide narrative assessments of student performance multiple times throughout the degree programs.	The Metropolitan curriculum is fully integrated at three levels: between the classroom and the workplace, across the semester's courses, and over time. While its highly structured curriculum is distinctive and not necessarily easily adaptable, it demonstrates well how working adults can experience an education that is much more than a collection of courses. Because Metropolitan was founded with integrative learning at its center, administrative support has been strong and continuous.

Examples That Foster Integrative Learning (cont.)

Example	Summary	Description	Commentary
Case Western Reserve University	*A purposeful pathway of integrative learning that culminates in a senior capstone*	The Seminar Approach to General Education and Scholarship (SAGES) recently became the core academic experience for all Case undergraduates. The four-year sequence begins with a first seminar that introduces students to the mission of the research university and to neighboring museums and institutes in Cleveland's University Circle. Next, each student takes two university seminars on topics ranging from Religious and Ethical Bodies to Nanoworlds. All first and university seminars are interdisciplinary and writing-intensive, and the curriculum is organized around a set of general themes (e.g., Thinking about the Social World, Thinking about the Symbolic World). In the third year, students enroll in departmental seminars which take SAGES's interactive, inquiry-based, and individualized approach to learning and apply it to study in the major disciplines. Finally, students complete a senior capstone in which they demonstrate the knowledge, problem-solving, and communication skills that they have acquired throughout their undergraduate careers. Many capstones effectively integrate theory with practice, as students apply their learning in professional and community placements.	Case Western Reserve has committed to providing all students a small-class, seminar experience in a large research university. SAGES stresses inquiry and integration, with the integration occurring across disciplines, over the college years, and between theory and practice. The structure builds a pathway from the freshman to the senior year, with the pedagogical methods purposefully chosen to advance the desired outcomes.

Examples That Foster Inquiry Learning

Example	Summary	Description	Commentary
The State of Washington	*A statewide high school capstone requirement in inquiry and integration*	Beginning with the class of 2008, the State of Washington will require high school graduates to complete a senior project that demonstrates senior-level competencies. These projects are described as including (1) a research paper, (2) a project that applies knowledge, (3) a student portfolio, and (4) a public presentation before a judging panel.	By requiring such a comprehensive senior-year exercise, the state will communicate to students, parents, and educators that the ability to frame an issue and justify an analysis is an expected outcome of high school. With proper support and implementation, senior projects will help students deepen and demonstrate inquiry and integrative capacities. Such a capstone project—building as it does on previous learning experiences in writing, finding information, and oral communication—will prepare students well for college.
Environmental and Spatial Technology Program (EAST)	*Service and project-based inquiry and integrative learning in high school*	The Environmental and Spatial Technology program (EAST), founded in 1995, was designed to engage high school students in collaborative, experiential, and service-based learning in a high-end software/hardware laboratory environment. It now involves more than two hundred high schools in seven states. The EAST model features dynamic, performance-based learning in which service-learning projects are integrated with advanced technological applications. The setting for the model is an interdisciplinary laboratory that focuses on the intellectual and problem-solving growth of students. Students—who in the EAST labs represent a mix of all achievement levels—create, design, and implement projects that assist the school and/or a community group. Students routinely apply learning from their other classes. At the end, many of them formally present their results to city or school councils, prepare written reports, or create multimedia packages that may include global satellite positioning data, high-end computer-assisted design, and other advanced-level science and mathematics. One EAST project involved testing well water quality over an entire county, identifying contaminated wells, and using	By participating in EAST, schools expand their ability to link traditional classroom learning to high-level inquiry-based projects. The students receive full and well-rounded experiential learning that advances integration and civic learning, as well as inquiry and team work, all in a stimulating high-tech environment.

Examples That Foster Inquiry Learning (cont.)

Example	Summary	Description	Commentary
EAST (cont.)		student-gathered GPS data and the computer to create an animated "fly-over" of the entire county that included well sites and topographical features. EAST programs are now also being explored for use with first-year college students.	
North Seattle Community College	*Inquiry in a community college through theme-based learning communities*	All students participate in a ten- to fifteen-credit, team-taught, and theme-based learning community focused on "discovering the interdisciplinary nature of knowledge" and "learning how to explore primary sources and other good books." By emphasizing student participation, collaboration, self-reflection, critical thinking, and writing, the courses foster structured dialogue around complex ideas, leading to the discovery of new knowledge. Themes, which mostly address cultural pluralism, have included Beginning: The Shaping of Cultures, Myths and Identities (perspectives from history, communication, literature, and women's studies). A regularly offered program, Ways of Knowing: How to Choose What to Believe, explores classical epistemological issues from different disciplinary perspectives.	In surveys, former students report that the learning communities were peak educational experiences. They praise the programs for building their knowledge, academic skills, confidence, motivation, and interest in civic engagement. Features of the learning communities that make them so successful include personal engagement with other students, challenging assignments, high expectations, interdisciplinary themes, and collaborative activities.
Alverno College	*Inquiry in a culture of formative assessment*	Alverno, a national leader in student assessment, bases its assessments on the products of active inquiry. The college's curriculum emphasizes how students are able to think and what they are able to do as a result of study in both general education and the major. Faculty members use their disciplines as frameworks for student learning and approach teaching as a process of engaging students in inquiry characteristic of those disciplines. Each department identifies those of the eight college-wide "abilities" that are most germane to inquiry in its field and then provides relevant learning and assessment opportunities. For example, study in the sciences emphasizes problem solving; the humanities stress aesthetic judgment. All disciplines focus on communication, analysis, and (usually) social interaction. Final assessments in major courses look at methods of inquiry, application, interaction, and communication that are central to the disciplines studied. For example, students in a small business course create a business plan that is assessed by both the course instructor and the loan officer of a local bank. Cell biology students engage in group research on cancer at the cellular level and present the results of their work both in writing and orally. Students in a course on literary criticism assume the role of a school district's curriculum council and, after a roundtable discussion on the merits of a selected novel, present an argument for or against including it in a high school English course. Feedback to the students is in the language of the abilities and disciplinary outcomes being assessed.	Transparency and disciplinary differences in inquiry characterize the Alverno approach. Since the curriculum is carefully constructed around the eight "abilities," which develop over time and across courses, students also experience inquiry in a developmental manner.
University of Maryland	*Freshman-and sophomore-level inquiry through discovery projects*	Discovery Projects are a feature of College Park Scholars, a residential learning community program enrolling 1,600 freshmen and sophomores. As one of three alternative activities, Discovery Projects introduce entering students to primary research that might take place at the nearby National Archives, but might also involve interviews, observations, content analysis, or field study. Students gather information on a topic of interest and ultimately present the "story" they discover as a collection of materials and as a poster for an academic showcase ending the school year. They also keep a logbook of reflections on the research process and the nature of knowledge.	The model rests on William Perry's theory of cognitive development and is designed to give students the balance of challenge and support that helps them move from dualistic to relativistic understandings. As one student noted, "Before this archives project, my idea of research was the compilation of other people's compilations. . . . Never before had I confronted the real thing—the original document, the memo, the press release, the confidential case file—and been forced to make the connections on my own. It was an amazing rush, having to figure things out for yourself like this."

Examples That Foster Inquiry Learning (cont.)

Example	Summary	Description	Commentary
North Carolina State University	*Widespread inquiry-guided learning in a research environment*	Work since 1999 has transformed undergraduate education at North Carolina State through the widespread and intentional introduction of "inquiry-guided learning," an approach identified as particularly relevant for research universities. The elements include the First-Year Inquiry Program—designated small seminar courses in many academic areas each of which develops critical reading and discussion skills and involves students in work with professors on timely topics. The first-year program aims both to instill in students a responsibility for their own learning and to develop strategies for increasingly moving from dichotomous thinking to more nuanced and complex considerations. It stresses critical thinking, active learning, and developing habits of independent inquiry. Subsequent courses, across the curriculum, continue attention to critical and synthetic thinking skills, collaborative learning, and the transfer of knowledge and skills from one domain to another. Departmental faculty have been designing purposeful pathways in the majors by identifying sequences of three or four courses that use inquiry-guided learning and relate developmentally to one another. The university also has a strong program of undergraduate student research.	North Carolina State has linked inquiry to its mission as a research university, an embodiment of intentional practice. Its comprehensive approach to inquiry in the academic departments will provide a transferable model as the faculty develops purposeful pathways.
The University of Nebraska–Lincoln	*A developmental approach to inquiry through student research*	With the resources of a large university available to them, students assist faculty members in research projects, benefiting from personalized expert advice and guidance during the research and through making public presentations of the results. Undergraduate Creative Activities and Research Experiences is a two-year program in which students spend the first year learning about research while serving as an assistant, and then the second designing and completing a project. The university provides financial support of up to $2,000 each for these research projects.	The unusual two-year program reflects an understanding that inquiry capacities, even through personal research experience, develop best over time.
Stanford University	*Inquiry through seminars and public service*	Stanford offers a rich array of inquiry-based opportunities for both lower- and upper-division students. Small enrollment introductory seminars provide lower-division students an opportunity to engage with faculty members in inquiry-based seminars on topics related to the instructor's interests. The Sophomore College engages second-year students in an intensive two and a half weeks of inquiry into particular topics preceding the beginning of the academic year. Like many large universities, Stanford offers extensive undergraduate research opportunities; one special feature, however, is the Public Service Scholars program of the Haas Center for Public Service, which supports seniors in writing their honors theses "as a form of public service."	Stanford is starting to create a purposeful pathway for developing skill in inquiry. The first- and second-year experiences prepare students well for advanced research in their major fields, which is supported through a variety of departmental and extra-departmental programs.

Examples That Foster Global Learning

Example	Summary	Description	Commentary
Lexington High School (Lexington, Massachusetts)	*A high school pathway in world history*	The school district requires middle school students to study world history in grade six and then world geography in grade seven. Building on this foundation of map-reading skills and general overview, high school students must complete world history (in grades nine and ten, with the latter course modeled on the AP world history curriculum). All this prepares them for the option of taking a wide array of junior/senior thematic electives, including The Holocaust and Other Genocides, Modern Japan, and International Relations: Human Rights. In addition, trips abroad, the Model United Nations Club, and national debates provide extracurricular reinforcement. The school system and the teachers support global education at all levels in the curriculum.	The school district has a nice pathway for students to engage with global issues. The study of foreign languages could also be linked with clear competency expectations by graduation. Ideally these expectations would align with those at college entry.
Community College of Philadelphia	*Multiple global opportunities and research abroad in a community college*	Students are given the option of following an international studies curriculum. This strong area studies program with a two-year foreign language requirement prepares them well for transfer to four-year institutions where they can continue with related courses or choose a globally focused major. In addition, the college offers short study abroad opportunities, including in London and Costa Rica, and a spring break educational experience in Mexico. A recent innovation in the five-week Costa Rica program has students completing social science fieldwork to improve both language and research skills. Topics in the undergraduate research component have included institutional care for the elderly and the role of women. After translation of the tape recordings and surveys, students write up their findings and present papers at regional academic conferences. The college has also expanded its foreign language offerings to include some lesser-taught languages not typically found in community colleges (e.g., Swahili and Hebrew). External grants have allowed faculty members to revise or create courses to stress global issues so that most students engage such issues several times in their two years. The general education reform now underway should increase the number of required international/global courses.	Through its various complementary initiatives, the college is building a learning culture infused with international study. This commitment is most unusual in the community college sector, where it is often thought difficult to provide global learning experiences for working adults and part-time students. However, since community colleges educate the overwhelming number of new immigrants and first-generation students, the demographic, ethnic, and linguistic diversity on these campuses enhance the environment for global learning. Many of the elements can form parts of purposeful pathways stretching between two- and four-year study. Clear learning outcomes enhance the intentionality of the college's offerings and should be part of new general education requirements. The new general education program could provide a crucial anchor for pathways in global learning.
Five College Supervised Independent Language Program	*A collaborative, inter-institutional approach to lesser-taught languages*	Run by the Five College Consortium, Inc., in Western Massachusetts, the Five College Center for the Study of World Languages coordinates a supervised independent language program which offers independent study in sixteen of the lesser-taught languages, including Czech, Hindi, Hungarian, and Wolof. The program allows motivated students with excellent language skills an opportunity to study languages not currently offered in classroom courses at Amherst College, Hampshire College, Mount Holyoke College, Smith College, or the University of Massachusetts, Amherst. Many students choose this approach to learning a "heritage" language. Recently, joint courses have also been offered in some languages utilizing a single instructor and multiparty interactive video classrooms installed on each campus. One of the center's goals is to facilitate the integration of less commonly taught languages into students' academic programs. By combining an elementary study of the language (through the center) with intensive intermediate/advanced study elsewhere or abroad, students can expand their global horizons and, at the same time, interweave that linguistic and cultural knowledge into a chosen academic specialty.	The approach is innovative in three ways. First, as a collaborative venture, it allows each institution to expand its students' access to language study. Second, it makes less commonly taught languages accessible to undergraduates at liberal arts colleges (four of the five institutions in the consortium are small liberal arts colleges). Third, it expands the concept of building on introductory language study through international experience. While it may be customary for art history students to perfect their Italian while studying in Florence, it is unusual for a journalism major to improve her Turkish by studying journalism in Istanbul.

Examples That Foster Global Learning (cont.)

Example	Summary	Description	Commentary
St. Lawrence University	*Learning communities to advance global, inquiry, and integrative learning*	All first-year students at St. Lawrence participate in theme-based residential learning communities designed to help them understand enduring global issues of worldwide significance. Themes such as "evolution of the American family" and "the cultural construction of communities" are pursued through multidisciplinary team-taught courses that emphasize writing, speaking, research, and critical reflection by employing problem-based approaches and collaborative learning. The emphases on diversity and global issues reflect St. Lawrence's perception of liberal education as preparation for responsible global leadership. Students may also elect to participate in upper-division living–learning communities. One such program has students living in a yurt village in the mountains while studying the social and natural history of the Adirondacks, comparative philosophies of human relations to nature, and expressive arts and nature.	The first-year learning communities exemplify the intersection of global, inquiry, and integrative learning. St. Lawrence has made a strong statement of commitment to these outcomes by requiring all students to participate.
Goucher College	*Required study abroad to advance global learning*	Enacting a key part of its strategic plan, Goucher will require all members of the graduating class of 2010 to participate in a study abroad program. Formats will range from three-week intensive courses to semester-long and yearlong programs. To help assure full participation, travel vouchers will be made available to all students. The study abroad requirement is one element of the college's stated strategic commitment to broadening international and intercultural awareness throughout the curriculum. Others include enhanced foreign language study and extensive curricular attention to cultures, diversity, and ecological sustainability.	The unique requirement could be an important touch-point in a pathway to global preparedness. Ideally it would be supported by an early introduction, some summative experience, and global issues across the curriculum. One assumes that the college plans to provide students comprehensive preparation before travel and meaningful opportunities to incorporate their experiences into subsequent formal study once they return to campus.
Drury University	*Global learning through a required core resulting in a global studies minor for all students*	The Global Perspectives 21 Curriculum enacts Drury's mission to "liberate persons to participate responsibly in and contribute to life in a global community." Through six courses emphasizing global issues over three years, students engage cultures, traditions, values, scientific inquiry, imagined futures, community building, and collaborative research. Electives with continued emphasis on global learning complete the program. Outcomes include facility with a second language; communication, reasoning, and problem-solving skills related to global issues; and substantial awareness and appreciation of other cultures.	Drury has instituted a mission-driven commitment to developing the global competency of all its graduates. Global learning not only infuses the core, it is the justification for the core—learning that prepares graduates for a new century of increasingly frequent international and intercultural encounters.
Kennesaw State University	*Global learning infused through-out a campus including in a core curriculum and senior capstone*	The required general education program emphasizes learning about cultural diversity and global interdependence through collaborative, multidisciplinary, and experiential courses. While general education is a modified distribution model, global issues form cross-cutting links. Many courses are expected to strengthen "understanding and critical thinking about world social issues" and "understanding of international and global perspectives." As part of general education, all students study world civilizations and world literature; even the American history course includes perspectives from other countries. Through an elective senior-year capstone experience, students construct electronic portfolios (referred to as "passports to global citizenship") that help them review, reflect on, and integrate their general education and major studies as they prepare to graduate as "global citizen leaders." Beyond the curriculum, annual performances, exhibits, and films related to a single country are brought to campus, intentionally adding global learning to the cocurriculum. Grants exist for faculty members to	At Kennesaw State, global issues infuse curricular and cocurricular programs, including much of general education. Creating such a climate is an especially effective model for an older, non-traditional student body like Kennesaw State's. The senior capstone provides a nice final "bookend" to a pathway that would be more purposeful if the general education program design elicited sequential development.

Examples That Foster Global Learning (cont.).

Example	Summary	Description	Commentary
Kennesaw State University (cont.)		write course modules on each year's featured country for both general education and major courses. The university voted to make "global learning for the engaged citizen" the focus of its upcoming accreditation.	
University of Delaware	*A threaded curriculum on global citizenship*	Liberal Education and Global Citizenship: The Arts of Democracy integrates courses, international discovery, service learning, technology, general education, the majors, and innovations in instruction, advising, and grading. Students select one of three global citizenship tracks: (1) Enacting Democracy, which explores the challenges facing the establishment, evolution, and operation of democratic forms of governance; (2) Global Community, which explores the similarities and differences across communities, highlighting local and individual issues and community responses; and (3) Transnational Issues, which explores the transnational forces—technology, environmental degradation, population growth and migration, arms trade, international human rights norms—that shape global action. The tracks begin in the freshman year, extend halfway into the sophomore year, and then are reinforced, extended, and expanded through upper-division activities, thereby providing a fully integrated, four-year global-citizenship experience. Each track has the same organization: a freshman-year thematic course selection and preparation with summer study abroad; a sophomore-year course/experience followed up with winter study abroad; a junior- and senior-year extension of thematic threads via course selection and cocurricular experience (internship, directed inquiry, study travel), culminating in a capstone project. Students also develop an electronic portfolio as a four-year, multimedia guide to the study of global citizenship. Participants accumulate points toward a global citizenship certificate awarded at graduation.	The structure allows for multiple exposures to the content of global learning over time. Clear articulation of the intended specific learning outcomes could even better help students see the intentionality of learning that informs the program.

Examples That Foster Civic Learning

Example	Summary	Description	Commentary
California High Schools–Cesar Chavez Day Curriculum	*A statewide, high school–level interdisciplinary approach to civic activism*	The Cesar Chavez Day curriculum, developed by the California Department of Education, uses history, cultural studies, geography, and civics to engage students with the life, work, and philosophy of Cesar Chavez. This dynamic program for grades ten through twelve has been used in schools throughout the state to address issues of social justice and social change through the example of one man's life. Intended to be sequential over the three years and taught on or around Cesar Chavez Day (March 3), the curriculum integrates new knowledge with what students have already learned in their classes. In grade ten, California requires the study of world history ending with a focus on the modern world and its social problems. The related Chavez curriculum augments the study of the Industrial Revolution by focusing on the role of labor unions, the reasons why Chavez started the United Farm Workers, and nonviolent social action modeled on Gandhi. In grade eleven, students learn about the history and growth of the United States; the Chavez curriculum explores agricultural practices, racial issues, and the beginnings of the civil rights movement through Chavez's work to improve the lives of farm workers. In grade twelve, emphasis is on principles of American democracy and a basic understanding of American capitalism; the complementary study is of how Chavez's ideas and actions provide a blueprint for engaged, active citizens.	This three-year, developmentally designed curriculum prepares students well for more advanced civic learning in college. It links the general and the specific, the national and the local.
Elisabeth Irwin High School (New York City)	*Civic learning in high school through local action and projects*	Elisabeth Irwin High School helped develop the Urban Citizenship project to prepare students for lives of active, informed, and effective citizenship. The project invites students to (1) identify and address critical urban issues that matter to them and to their communities; (2) share their viewpoints and publish their own work; (3) engage in online dialogue and debate both with peers and with members of political and civil society, locally and across the globe; and (4) engage in meaningful urban planning, policy development, and civic action with expert mentors from government and civil society. As one example, in 2003, the project hosted a conference, "Re-Imagining New York," which sought to involve students in the process of revitalizing the city, focusing especially on the area surrounding the World Trade Center site. Students from public and private schools worked alongside political and civic leaders, scholars, community activists, architects, and urban planners. They learned from experts in economic development, environmental impact, housing, education, and transportation; met with residents of Lower Manhattan; and studied how other cities around the world recovered from cataclysmic events. Ultimately, they developed their own ideas for a new downtown and designed a memorial.	Much of what passes for civics education in K–12 is remote from the lives of students; this comprehensive program engages their interest by involving them in local issues.
Constitutional Rights Foundation— Active Citizenship Today Program	*Externally designed course modules that advance civic and integrative learning in schools through service, inquiry, and research*	The Constitutional Rights Foundation, in conjunction with Close Up Foundation, has designed Active Citizenship Today (ACT). This curriculum, which includes service learning, fosters civic responsibility by teaching young people how to participate effectively in a democracy. Through a curriculum developed for grades six through twelve, ACT links in-depth study of civics with active community involvement. Students learn about the people, processes, and institutions involved in improving community conditions; develop skills to participate in policy making; and cultivate positive attitudes toward lifelong service for the common good. The ACT program takes students through five related and sequential units of study. In unit 1, they examine community resources and problems; in unit 2, they choose and research a community problem; in unit 3, they analyze and evaluate policy; in unit 4, they explore options for working on a community problem; and in the concluding unit 5, they bring their learning and experience together to plan, implement, and evaluate a student-directed project. The ACT modules are intended to fit with any U.S. government, contemporary American problems, or community-service course.	The developmental program nicely advances three of the outcomes—civic, inquiry, and integrative learning—through service and research. It positions students well to continue building on the middle school and high school experiences when they enter college.

Examples That Foster Civic Learning (cont.)

Example	Summary	Description	Commentary
University of Hawai'i, Kapi'olani Community College	*Intensive service learning at a community college*	Service learning is one of the college's six major cross-curricular emphases; as such, it is integrated into at least fifty courses each semester, across all programs. Collaboratively developed outcomes, assessments, and partnership principles help faculty members to integrate service learning into their courses. Students are encouraged to test and apply theories learned in the classroom to community work. Critical reflective journaling links the service to on-campus study. A number of service-learning pathways enable students to continue their community involvement across multiple semesters and even once they transfer to the University of Hawai'i Manoa campus. The pathways include both community-based options (e.g., promoting health and preventing HIV/AIDS, environmental sustainability) and school-based options (e.g., English language tutoring; enrichment in arts, music, and science). The pathways are being aligned with United Nations Millennium goals to make explicit links between local and global learning.	At Kapi'olani, service learning to advance diversity and civic engagement has become a feature of the institution; it is no longer an innovation at the margins. The pathways allow theory–practice and local–global linkages to deepen.
California State University, Monterey Bay	*Clear learning outcomes of a required, two-step service-learning program*	Monterey Bay is committed to education as a process of learning how to make meaning and create one's own knowledge. Believing such learning should be active and engaged, the university has created a service-learning institute whose mission is to promote social justice by cultivating reciprocal service and learning partnerships among students, faculty, staff, and members of the surrounding community. The institute is housed in the College of University Studies and Programs. It serves as an instructional unit, an academic resource center, a center for developing community partnerships, and the home of an innovative student leadership program. The curricular element requires that students complete a two-step program for graduation. Transparent and well-articulated learning outcomes describe what students are expected to know and be able to do at the end of the program. These outcomes fall into the categories of justice, compassion, diversity, and social responsibility (e.g., students will be able to understand the social realities and life choices available to different individuals and social groups; students will develop skills as multicultural community builders, able to interact sensitively with diverse populations). All students must fulfill two components: in the lower division, an approved service-learning course from a short list; and in the upper division, a service-learning course that meets the requirements of the major (e.g., in business, management of nonprofit organizations; in earth science, interpreting Monterey Bay natural history for the community).	Civic learning at Monterey Bay is unusual in many ways: it is supported by a special institute, it is characterized by very clear learning outcomes; it is fostered by a two-step curriculum; it links civic engagement to the majors; it keeps civic involvement at the heart of its academic work; and it is required for graduation.
The College of New Jersey	*Civic, inquiry, and integrative learning through community-based research and service*	The Trenton Youth Community-Based Research Corps is an interdisciplinary program dedicated to serving the research needs of local social service agencies while also educating undergraduate students in applied research and social justice. Over three semesters, a small group of students works with a faculty mentor and community partners. Students learn to think critically and contextually about—and undertake action to address—issues related to inner-city children, adolescents, and families. They develop skills in applied research, leadership, community development, and youth advocacy. As a community–campus collaboration, the interdisciplinary foundational course, Downtown: Inner-City Youth and Families, aims to stimulate awareness of the complex lives of inner-city youths and families, particularly those who live in poverty. Next, students enroll in a two-semester research sequence to conduct community-based research in collaboration with the faculty mentor and a Trenton social service agency serving youths and families. The program culminates in professional reports and public presentations, student coauthored manuscripts submitted to scholarly journals, and a "community reflection portfolio" for each student.	Community-based research programs—while extremely powerful means to advance civic, inquiry, and integrative learning—depend on systemic, sustained support beyond resources normally available to courses (e.g., direct project costs, mechanisms for student academic and faculty teaching credit). The active development and maintenance of community partnerships requires time and attention. Because academic and community schedules do not necessarily coincide, work may need to be done beyond the boundaries of the typical academic semester.

Examples That Foster Civic Learning (cont.)

Example	Summary	Description	Commentary
Indiana University	*Sequential and integrative civic learning culminating in a community-based capstone project*	The five-course minor in leadership, ethics, and social action begins in the sophomore year with an introductory course that includes two hours of volunteer service per week. Courses in ethics, social organization, and social action follow, each selected from a very short list of possibilities. The minor, organized for students in any major, culminates in a senior capstone for three to six credits in which the student completes a project designed to address a need expressed by a cooperating community agency. A faculty member serves as adviser for the capstone project and assists as the student gathers bibliographic material, formulates appropriate questions, and connects the community-based project with relevant scholarship. Ideally, the project would tie together the student's major field of study with community needs.	With a community placement focused on strengthening learning in the student's major, this minor in civic learning is a model that could broadly appeal to students and departments at many campuses. The minor's pathway of learning prepares students for significant service to the community.
Duke University	*Service-learning pathways, research, and a capstone to advance civic learning, inquiry, and integration*	"Research service learning" that links academic knowledge, ethical inquiry, and civic leadership characterizes the new initiative called Scholarship with a Civic Mission. In this developmental and progressive model, students, faculty members, and community partners study questions of shared interest. Research, conducted in the context of a service-learning experience, is part of the service to the community. The model begins with a gateway course that introduces ethical issues and research skills while providing a service-learning experience. It is followed by a research opportunity that could be an independent study or a field-based internship; the work unfolds through collaboration with community partners in a local, national, or international setting. Students undertake critical reflection on the intellectual, ethical, and civic issues revealed. The final stage is a capstone (course, independent study, or honors seminar) in which students pursue a research project that builds on the former collaborations. At the end, they publicly present their findings and share the results with the community. Completion of the three stages confers the designation of Duke Civic Scholar. The research service-learning pathways can be based within an academic discipline or connect several disciplines through a theme. External grants support student participation.	Duke's new program cleverly reflects a research university's commitment to the discovery of new knowledge; it links this traditional mission with a new awareness of civic mission. The design advances cumulative learning in three important outcome areas: civic, inquiry, and integrative learning. The purposeful pathway model, with its structured process of critical reflection, can also serve to generate evidence for assessment purposes.

Assessing the Four Outcomes

TO ASSESS THE FOUR LEARNING OUTCOMES ADDRESSED IN THIS PUBLICATION—or any others resulting from a practical, engaged liberal education—a campus would need to follow the steps more fully explained in *The Art and Science of Assessing General Education Outcomes* (Leskes and Wright 2005). It would begin by defining the outcomes, formulating questions to answer (including a decision about the levels of analysis—see Miller and Leskes 2005), selecting methods, gathering evidence of student learning, analyzing the evidence, and closing the loop by using the findings to improve the teaching/learning process.

As already mentioned, the forum's reflective seminars unearthed few good examples of assessments designed with integrative, inquiry, global, and civic learning in mind. However, with greater frequency, one now can find both assignments and rubrics that reveal whether and how well students are achieving the objectives of these four learning outcomes. This last chapter includes two good assessment examples for each outcome (or an aspect of each). Because the campus of origin has described the desired learning in its own way, the criteria may not perfectly align with the definitions in chapter 3. However, collectively these eight examples give an idea of how learning even of complex capacities can be rigorously assessed.

Each featured assignment and/or rubric could easily be modified or adapted; it could be used at a different level of analysis or further refined. Holistic assessments could be made more analytical if faculty members were to tease out and explicate the relevant behaviors. The descriptions include the context of each assessment, the criteria, and a rating scale for determining quality. In the interest of brevity, the authors have reformatted the originals and often excerpted from them. The hierarchy proposed in chapter 2 (see sidebar) is used to characterize the examples.

Assessment of Integrative Learning

Integrative learning includes many powerful abilities ranging from noticing connections to solving complex problems by drawing on many sources. Therefore, assessments for integrative learning will vary greatly: the least complex may simply acknowledge the presence of integrative behaviors, while more analytical assessment may focus on particular manifestations of integration. In all cases, the capacities desired will determine both the integrative experiences and their assessments. In research related to assessment of integrative learning, Mansilla (2005) interviewed practitioners to uncover factors critical to assessment of interdisciplinary work, including integrative factors.

Source: **Bowling Green State University**

Title: Levels of Connection

Context: Rubric is provided institution-wide to facilitate assessment of integration in any discipline. Faculty members are encouraged to adopt or adapt the rubric for use in their own courses and projects.

Description: A four-level, holistic rubric with each level containing descriptions of multiple integrative behaviors. There is a fairly clear sense of increasing sophistication and complexity in the move from the beginner to advanced levels. In the hierarchy of assessments, this would be a level 2 or 3, depending upon the work examined and its relationship to the central outcomes of the assignments or experiences.

Level	Criteria
4 (Advanced)	▪ identifies ways to reconcile diverse or conflicting priorities, viewpoints, or options ▪ calls attention to something that has not been adequately noticed by others (e.g., a subtle or deep relationship, novel findings or interpretations, the context or frame of reference) ▪ applies frameworks from multiple domains of knowledge and practice to create something (e.g., business plan, musical composition, thesis, capstone paper, research project) ▪ integrates diverse elements into a product, performance, or artifact that fits its context coherently
3 (Proficient)	▪ uses disciplinary frameworks and concepts to illuminate relationships among apparently diverse items ▪ examines phenomena from multiple viewpoints, both concretely and abstractly ▪ specifies the limits or boundaries within which generalizations apply ▪ applies abstract academic knowledge to solve concrete practical problems
2 (Novice)	▪ organizes groups of items into ordered collections and specifies the organizing principle(s) ▪ recognizes links among topics and concepts presented in different courses ▪ relates and uses information from other courses or experiences in the current setting ▪ formulates generalizations about collections or sets of items ▪ distinguishes concrete and abstract representations ▪ identifies disciplinary concepts (theories, frameworks) and instances of their application
1 (Beginner)	▪ describes similarities and differences in a collection or set of items ▪ categorizes items or observations into groups ▪ recognizes simple links among topics or concepts in a course ▪ offers accurate definitions of terms and concepts ▪ describes the setting (e.g., context, environment, culture, domain) in which connections are being made

Source: **California State University, Fresno**

Title: General Education Scoring Guide for Integrative Arts and Humanities

Context: Used to assess student work in upper-division courses that fulfill a university integration requirement.

Description: The work products are assessed in two areas—integration and discipline—with short descriptions of the quality expected. The rubric can be used holistically to produce a single score for the two areas combined or more analytically to produce a score in each area. This could be a level 5 assessment if the scores for integration and the discipline were reported separately.

Level	Integration	Discipline
4 - Accomplished	■ successfully integrates interdisciplinary skills and knowledge ■ demonstrates a high degree of intellectual acuity, imagination, and sensitivity ■ clearly demonstrates an awareness of interrelationships among self, the discipline, society, and culture	■ clearly and reflectively applies appropriate argumentation and methodology of the discipline ■ demonstrates highly innovative interpretations, perspectives, or applications of course content
3 - Competent	■ partially integrates interdisciplinary skills and knowledge ■ demonstrates intellectual acuity, imagination, and sensitivity ■ demonstrates some awareness of interrelationships among self, the discipline, society, and culture	■ applies appropriate argumentation and methodology of the discipline ■ demonstrates coherent interpretations, perspectives, or applications of course content
2 - Developing	■ attempts to integrate interdisciplinary skills and knowledge ■ lacks depth of intellectual acuity, imagination, and sensitivity ■ demonstrates little awareness of interrelationships among self, the discipline, society, and culture	■ attempts appropriate argumentation and methodology of the discipline ■ offers minimal interpretations, perspectives, or applications of course content
1 - Does not meet minimum objectives	■ does not yet integrate interdisciplinary skills and knowledge ■ does not yet demonstrate intellectual acuity, imagination, and sensitivity ■ does not yet demonstrate awareness of interrelationships among self, the discipline, society, and culture	■ does not incorporate appropriate argumentation and methodology of the discipline ■ fails to interpret or apply course content

Assessment of Inquiry Learning

Assessment of inquiry can be challenging given the complex behaviors represented by the term. However, critical thinking is often cited as an important aspect of inquiry, and numerous assessments exist for this ability (some locally and others externally developed). Following are two assessments for critical thinking with somewhat contrasting approaches. The Collegiate Learning Assessment, a standardized performance assessment of critical thinking, is another option (see www.cae.org).

Source: **Insight Assessment**, developed by Facione and Facione

Title: Holistic Critical Thinking Scoring Rubric
The following is a slightly modified version. (See www.insightassessment.com/HCTSR. html to obtain a full rubric packet that also contains cover page, class rating form, and instructions. Similar rubrics directly addressing the intended learning outcomes of general education are available for free download from www.insightassessment.com/free_ tools.html.)

Context: Scores critical thinking in student essays, portfolios, or projects. The authors specifically suggest training to ensure consistent scoring by multiple readers.

Description: Holistic rubric with four levels and multiple descriptors. The top two levels contain positive and the lower two negative statements. This is a level 2 or level 3 assessment, depending upon the nature of the assignment scored.

Score	Criteria	Behaviors
4	Consistently does all or almost all of the following:	■ accurately interprets evidence, statements, graphics, questions, etc. ■ identifies the salient arguments (reasons and claims) pro and con ■ thoughtfully analyzes and evaluates major alternative points of view ■ draws warranted, judicious, non-fallacious conclusions ■ fair-mindedly follows where evidence and reasons lead
3	Does most or many of the following:	■ accurately interprets evidence, statements, graphics, questions, etc. ■ identifies relevant arguments (reasons and claims) pro and con ■ offers analyses and evaluations of obvious alternative points of view ■ draws warranted, non-fallacious conclusions ■ fair-mindedly follows where evidence and reasons lead
2	Does most or many of the following:	■ misinterprets evidence, statements, graphics, questions, etc. ■ fails to identify strong, relevant counterarguments ■ ignores or superficially evaluates obvious alternative points of view ■ draws unwarranted or fallacious conclusions ■ regardless of the evidence or reasons, maintains or defends views
1	Consistently does all or almost all of the following:	■ offers biased interpretations of evidence, statements, graphics, questions, information, or points of view of others ■ fails to identify or hastily dismisses strong, relevant counterarguments ■ ignores or superficially evaluates obvious alternative points of view ■ argues using fallacious or irrelevant reasons and unwarranted claims ■ regardless of the evidence or reasons, maintains or defends views ■ exhibits close-mindedness or hostility to reason

Source: **University of Michigan, Flint**

Title: Scoring Rubric for Critical Thinking

(See assessment.umflint.edu/GeneralEducation/documents/Critical%20Thinking2.pdf.)

Context: The College of Arts and Sciences assesses essays written for a freshman-level introduction to college course and by a random sample of seniors participating in an assessment day. After reading a 300-400 word essay that makes a recommendation for action (such as voting for a particular person or proposition), students write a 150-200 word critical analysis of the argument contained in the original essay. A cross-disciplinary committee reads and scores all the essays.

Description: Analytical rubric with fourteen assessment areas, each scored on a scale of 1–4. The college expects at least half of the essays to score a 3 (good) or higher in each area. This is a level 5 assessment.

Outcome	Evidence of Outcome The Student . . .	Score Each Area 4 (Outstanding) 3 (Good) 2 (Adequate) 1 (Unacceptable)
Students will demonstrate the ability to take reasoned positions on issues of importance and support those positions with evidence	■ has a clearly stated conclusion as to the reasonableness of the argument in the author's essay ■ provides reasons to support his/her conclusion 　　the reasons are relevant 　　the reasons are adequate	
Students will demonstrate the ability to apply reasoning to solve authentic problems through experimentation, data collection, and induction of principles	■ accurately interprets statistical data in charts and/or tables ■ draws appropriate conclusions from the statistical data in charts and/or tables	
Students will demonstrate the ability to apply quantitative reasoning to problem solving	■ demonstrates an understanding of what role the statistical (quantitative) evidence plays in the author's argument ■ demonstrates an ability to critically assess the relevance of the quantitative evidence ■ demonstrates an ability to critically assess the accuracy of the quantitative evidence	
Students will demonstrate the ability to critically examine issues that affect their world	■ identifies the conclusion (the main point) of the author's essay ■ identifies the reason(s) (the evidence) offered by the author in support of that conclusion ■ identifies an implication (or implications) of accepting the author's proposal ■ evaluates the implications of accepting the author's proposal ■ provides reason(s) to support his/her assessment of the implication of the author's proposal	

Assessment of Global Learning

Global learning includes both on- and off-campus experiences. As campuses develop purposeful pathways for global learning, relevant assessment will become more common. Both of the following assessments were designed for use with on-campus experiences. As global learning efforts move beyond Western/non-Western and self/other paradigms, models for assessment should reflect those changed emphases.

Source: **Buffalo State University**

Title: Other World Civilizations Rubric
(See www.buffalostate.edu/offices/assessment/gened.htm#.)

Context: A random sample of written assignments is collected from courses designated as fulfilling the Other World Civilizations requirement of the general education program. The resulting scores, obtained from ratings by two professors who teach in the separate Western Civilization category, serve to assess the program, not individual students.

Description: Multifactor scoring statements in four levels produce a holistic score. This is a level 3 assessment.

Level	Criteria
4	▪ analysis and synthesis marked by distinctive use of detail to shape the analysis ▪ exhibits insight as to the interactions of distinctive features of the civilization ▪ understands distinctive features or components of a non-Western civilization within an appropriate temporal or spatial context ▪ recognizes salient features or components of a non-Western civilization, but without context
3	▪ exhibits insight as to the interactions of distinctive features of the civilization ▪ understands distinctive features or components of a non-Western civilization within an appropriate temporal or spatial context ▪ recognizes salient features or components of a non-Western civilization, but without context
2	▪ understands distinctive features or components of a non-Western civilization within an appropriate temporal or spatial context ▪ recognizes salient features or components of a non-Western civilization, but without context
1	▪ recognizes salient features or components of non-Western civilization, but without context

Source: **University of Arkansas–Fort Smith**

Title: Global and Cultural Perspectives
(See www.uafortsmith.edu/Learning/GlobalAndCulturalPerspectives.)

Context: The university developed the rubric for program assessment of the Global and Cultural Perspectives category of general education. A committee is assigned to monitor each of the ten general education competency categories which are assessed on a rotating basis. Students write an essay in response to prompts and/or a reading on a global topic.

Description: Assessment examines two student behaviors, with four levels of quality each. The two behaviors can also be combined for an assessment of the overarching outcome. The rubric was designed with the idea that students would progress through each of the four quality levels during their four college years. This is a level 5 assessment.

Overarching Outcome: Students differentiate between their own personal values and the value systems of others when interacting with groups of various backgrounds		
Level of behavior	**Student Behavior One** The student compares and contrasts characteristics of his/her own culture with those of other cultures	**Student Behavior Two** The student appraises contributions made to literature, science, politics, and the arts by a variety of cultures
Exemplary	■ synthesizes a variety of beliefs and behaviors gathered from multiple cultural backgrounds	■ analyzes why some contributions are adopted while others are rejected
Accomplished	■ objectively explains the difference in cultural perspectives	■ recognizes ways in which other cultures have great contributions that have not been adopted by one's own culture
Developing	■ recognizes the variety of cultural perspectives outside of one's own life	■ identifies specific contributions from other cultures that are present in one's own culture
Beginning	■ recognizes the dominant cultural perspective in one's own life	■ recognizes that all cultures have made significant contributions

Assessment of Civic Learning

Civic learning is multidimensional; it can be fostered in many different ways, some of which involve experiences away from campus. As institutions clarify their expectations in civic learning, assessment methods and rubrics will need to adapt to multiple venues. The first assessment example below emphasizes social responsibility, and the second examines ethics of social responsibility, from a program utilizing off-campus experiences.

Source: **Dordt College**[6]

Title: Student Assessment Essay: Recognition/Application of Perspectives (See www.dordt.edu/publications/assessment/apdxb.shtml.)

Context: Students are asked to write essays on social challenges twice, during their first and last years. Each essay is completed in fifty minutes—as part of orientation for freshmen and an assessment day (designed for gathering data on social responsibility) for seniors.

Description: The rubric provides both a holistic score for the entire essay and analytic scores for each ability area. Somewhat unique is the use of several scores (e.g., 3, 4, or 5) for single scoring statement areas. This is a level 5 assessment.

---

[6]The assessment example from Dordt College was also used in *The Art and Science of Assessing General Education Outcomes* (Leskes and Wright 2005).

Scoring criteria	1 2	3 4 5	6 7
Forms of moral judgment	■ external authorities, arbitrary view of right and wrong ■ doing what you're told	■ internalized authorities, knows answers but not sure why ■ right and wrong depend on/ relative to situation	■ attempts to understand and articulate norms and principles derived from internalized understanding of the value implications of one's faith commitment
Worldview	■ simplistic ■ not aware of having a worldview as explicit and interrelated system of beliefs, assumptions, and commitments	■ worldview consists primarily of a synthesis of conventional beliefs, assumptions, and morals ■ little evidence of reflection on the more generalized implications of assumptions, beliefs, or commitments	■ awareness of one's worldview as explicit system based on a deliberate, conscious affirmation of values, assumptions, beliefs, and commitments ■ can evaluate others' systems from this vantage point
Acceptance of personal responsibility in response to challenges	■ not my problem ■ shows little empathy ■ situation judged in terms of own needs and concerns ■ simplistic solutions without evidence of personal commitment to action	■ aware of personal impact and need for involvement ■ unclear as to the nature and extent of communal responsibility and action ■ solutions/suggestions are broader in scope, but not comprehensive	■ clearly sees self as involved and responsible for dealing with issues in concrete, clearly articulated ways ■ sensitive to the broader communal impact of individual action
Historical/structural basis	■ no mention or acknowledgment of historical development or impact of societal structures ■ problems based exclusively on personal responsibility	■ mentions historical development and/or societal structures, but focus is on personal, immediate, or situational influences	■ explicitly states that problems often have a historical context, and that societal or cultural structures contribute to individual and societal problems

Source: **Tusculum College**

Title: Ethics of Social Responsibility

(See www.tusculum.edu/academics/civicarts/competency/comp_ethics.html.)

Context: Tusculum has identified "foundation" and "practice of virtue" competencies. Every course develops at least one such competency resulting in multiple occasions for collecting assessment evidence over the span of a degree program. Ethics of Social Responsibility is one of three "practice of virtue" competencies (along with self-knowledge and civility). Level 2 achievement is the goal for graduation, with level 3 considered honors work. Criteria appear in every syllabus, becoming increasingly rigorous (advancing from level 1 to level 2) as students move from lower- to upper-division courses.

Description: Three levels of competency are described for four specific areas of the outcome. This is an example of a level 5 assessment.

Scoring criteria	Level 1	Level 2	Level 3
Individual and community	■ demonstrates awareness of interdependence of individual and community	■ demonstrates understanding of ethical issues generated by interdependence of individual and community, and mutual dependence of groups within a community	■ demonstrates commitment to balancing ethical demands of individuals and community and of groups within a community
Public and private life	■ can distinguish between public and private realms	■ recognizes appropriate speech and action for both public and private space ■ demonstrates understanding that actions in the public realm may have consequences for the private realm, and vice versa	■ demonstrates commitment to balancing boundaries of public and private responsibility so that appropriate action and interaction are possible in both
Diversity and the common good	■ demonstrates tolerance of diversity and cultural difference ■ acknowledges possibility of seeking common ground	■ shows willingness to suspend own beliefs for a time in order to learn about others ■ demonstrates sensitivity to diversity and cultural difference ■ shows willingness to seek common good	■ demonstrates commitment to a climate of diversity and cultural difference ■ shows willingness to suspend, examine, and possibly modify own beliefs within such a climate ■ shows commitment to seeking common good
Civic responsibility and social change	■ shows understanding of process of social change in a democratic system	■ demonstrates understanding of complexity of social change and of responsibility of citizens as agents of change in a democratic system	■ demonstrates commitment to participating in community as a citizen ■ shows ability to recognize ethical problems within a system and address them by seeking to initiate change in a responsible manner

References

Note: Internet addresses in the text are current as of August 2006

Accreditation Board for Engineering and Technology, Inc. 2000. *Criteria for accrediting engineering programs*. Baltimore, MD: Accreditation Board for Engineering and Technology, Inc.

Association of American Colleges. 1991. *The challenge of connecting learning: Project on liberal learning, study-in-depth, and the arts and sciences major*. Washington, DC: Association of American Colleges.

Association of American Colleges and Universities. 1995. *The drama of diversity and democracy: Higher education and American commitments*. Washington, DC: Association of American Colleges and Universities.

——. 2002. *Greater expectations: A new vision for learning as a nation goes to college*. Washington, DC: Association of American Colleges and Universities.

——. 2004. *Taking responsibility for the quality of the baccalaureate degree*. Washington, DC: Association of American Colleges and Universities.

——. 2005a. *Liberal education outcomes: A preliminary report on student achievement in college*. Washington, DC: Association of American Colleges and Universities.

——. 2005b. *Our students' best work: A framework for accountability worthy of our mission*. Washington, DC: Association of American Colleges and Universities.

Astin, A., L. Vogelgesang, E. Ikeda, and J. Yee. 2000. *How service learning affects students* (executive summary). Los Angeles: Higher Education Research Institute.

Avens, C., and R. Zelley. 1992. *QUANTA: An interdisciplinary learning community (four studies)*. Daytona Beach: Daytona Beach Community College (ERIC Document Reproduction Service No. ED349 073).

Belenky, M., B. Clinchy, N. Goldberger, and J. Tarule. 1986. *Women's ways of knowing*. New York: Basic Books.

Bereiter, C., and M. Scardamalia. 1989. Intentional learning as a goal of instruction. In L. B. Resnick, ed. *Knowing, learning, and instruction*. Hillsdale, NJ: Erlbaum, 361–92.

Bransford, J. D., A. L. Brown, and R. R. Cocking. 2000. *How people learn: Brain, mind, experience, and school*. Washington, DC: National Academy Press.

Brower, A. 1997. *End-of-year evaluation on the Bradley Learning Community*. Unpublished report, University of Wisconsin–Madison.

Bruner, J. 1960. *The process of education*. Cambridge, MA: Harvard University Press.

Business–Higher Education Forum. 1999. *Spanning the chasm: A blueprint for action*. Washington, DC: ACE/National Alliance of Business.

Education Commission of the States. 2000. *Every student a citizen: Creating the democratic self*. Denver: Education Commission of the States.

The Education Trust–West. 2002. *The high school diploma: Making it more than an empty promise*. Prepared for Senate Standing Committee on Education hearing on Senate Bill 1731, April.

Gardiner, L. F. 1994. *Redesigning higher education: Producing dramatic gains in student learning*. ASHE-ERIC Higher Education Report 23 (7). Washington, DC: The George Washington University, Graduate School of Education and Human Development.

Halpern, D. F., and M. D. Hakel. 2003. Applying the science of learning to the university and beyond: Teaching for long-term retention and transfer. *Change* 35 (4): 2–13.

Hovland, K. 2006. *Shared futures: Global learning and liberal education*. Washington, DC: Association of American Colleges and Universities.

Huber, M. T., and P. Hutchings. 2004. *Integrative learning: Mapping the terrain*. Washington, DC: Association of American Colleges and Universities.

Jacoby, B. 1996. *Service-learning in higher education: Concepts and practices*. San Francisco: Jossey–Bass.

Johnson, D. W., R. T. Johnson, and K. A. Smith. 1991. *Cooperative learning: Increasing college faculty instructional productivity*. ASHE-FRIC Higher Education Report No.4. Washington, D.C.: School of Education and Human Development, George Washington University.

Johnson, J. L., and S. King. 1997. Russell scholars program: Evaluation of the inaugural year. Unpublished report, University of Southern Maine.

Kegan, R. 1982. *The evolving self: Problem and process in human development*. Cambridge, MA: Harvard University Press.

King, P., and K. Kitchner. 1994. *Developing reflective judgment: Understanding and promoting intellectual growth and critical thinking in adolescents and adults*. San Francisco: Jossey-Bass.

Klein, J. 1999. *Mapping interdisciplinary studies*. Washington, DC: Association of American Colleges and Universities.

Knefelkamp, L., C. Widick, and C. Parker. 1978. *Applying new developmental findings*. San Francisco: Jossey-Bass.

Knefelkamp, L., and J. Cornfeld. 1979. Combining student stages and style in the design of learning environments. Paper presented at the annual meeting of the American College Personnel Association, Los Angeles.

Kolb, D. 1983. *Experiential learning: Experience as the source of learning and development*. Upper Saddle River, NJ: Prentice Hall.

Leskes, A., and B. D. Wright. 2005. *The art and science of assessing general education outcomes*. Washington, DC: Association of American Colleges and Universities.

Mansilla, V. B. 2005. Assessing student work at disciplinary crossroads. *Change* 37 (1): 14–21.

Mazur, L. A., and S. E. Sechler. 1997. *Global interdependence and the need for social stewardship*. New York: Rockefeller Brothers Fund.

McKeachie, W. J., P. R. Pintrich, Y. Lin, D. A. F. Smith, and R. Sharma. 1990. *Teaching and learning in the college classroom: A review of the research literature*. Ann Arbor, MI: National Center for Research to Improve Postsecondary Teaching and Learning.

Miller, R., and A. Leskes. 2005. *Levels of assessment: From the student to the institution*. Washington, DC: Association of American Colleges and Universities.

Musil, C. M. 2003. Educating for citizenship. *Peer Review* 5 (3): 4–8.

———. 2006. *Assessing global learning: Matching good intentions with good practice*. Washington, DC: Association of American Colleges and Universities.

National Council of Teachers of Mathematics. 2000. *Principles and standards for school mathematics*. Reston, VA: National Council of Teachers of Mathematics.

Oates, K., and L. Leavitt. 2003. *Service-learning and learning communities: Tools for integration and assessment*. Washington, DC: Association of American Colleges and Universities.

Pascarella, E. T., and P. T. Terenzini. 1991. *How college affects students: Findings and insights from twenty years of research*. San Francisco: Jossey-Bass.

Perry, W. G., Jr. 1999. *Forms of intellectual and ethical development in the college years: A scheme*. San Francisco: Jossey-Bass.

Ratcliff, J. L. 1997. Quality and coherence in general education. In J. G. Gaff, J. L. Ratcliff, and Associates, eds. *Handbook of the undergraduate curriculum: A comprehensive guide to purposes, structures, practices, and change*. San Francisco: Jossey-Bass.

Schneider, C. G. 2003. Preparing students for what? School–college alignment in an era of greater expectations. *Peer Review* 5 (2): 13–16.

Tinto, V., A. G. Love, and P. Russo. 1994. *Building learning communities for new college students: A summary of research findings of the Collaborative Learning Project*. University Park, PA: National Center on Postsecondary Teaching, Learning, and Assessment.

U.S. Department of Education. 1998. *Goals 2000: Reforming education to improve student achievement*. Washington, DC: U.S. Department of Education.

Vygotsky, L. 1978. *Mind in society: The development of higher psychological processes*. Cambridge, MA: Harvard University Press.

Woods, D. R. 1987. How might I teach problem solving? In J. E. Stice, ed. *Developing critical thinking and problem-solving abilities*. New Directions for Teaching and Learning. San Francisco: Jossey-Bass.

Working Group Members*

Working Group on Inquiry Learning

John Harris, Associate Provost for Quality Assessment
Samford University

Sharon Hamilton, Chancellor's Professor of English
Indiana University–Purdue University Indianapolis

Madelaine Marquez, Director, Center for
Innovative Education
Hampshire College

David Ruff, Director of School Reform
Southern Maine Partnership
University of Southern Maine

Nancy Shapiro, Associate Vice Chancellor,
Academic Affairs
University System of Maryland

Robert Shoenberg, chair, Senior Fellow
AAC&U

Barbara Leigh Smith, Codirector, National Learning
Communities Project
The Evergreen State College

Working Group on Integrative Learning

Deborah DeZure, Director of Faculty and Organizational
Development, and Senior Adviser to the Provost
Michigan State University

Scott Evenbeck, Dean, University College
Indiana University–Purdue University Indianapolis

Roy Garcia, Principal
South Grand Prairie High School
South Grand Prairie, Texas

Helen F. Giles-Gee, Provost
Rowan University

Lynne Gilli, Program Manager
Career and Technology Education Instructional Branch
Maryland State Department of Education

Beverlye Horton, Academy Facilitator
South Grand Prairie High School
South Grand Prairie, Texas

Debra Humphreys, cochair, Vice President for
Communications and Public Affairs
AAC&U

Julie Thompson Klein, Professor of Humanities
Department of Interdisciplinary Studies
Wayne State University

Ross Miller, cochair, Director of Programs
Office for Education and Quality Initiatives
AAC&U

Richard Vaz, Associate Dean of Interdisciplinary
and Global Studies
Worcester Polytechnic Institute

Working Group on Global Learning

Terry Bigalke, Dean of Academic Programs
East–West Center (Honolulu)

Michele Forman, 2001 National Teacher of the Year
Social Studies
Middlebury Union High School
Middlebury, Vermont

Madeleine Green, Vice President and Director
of International Initiatives
American Council on Education

Barbara Hill, chair, Senior Fellow
AAC&U

John Hudzik, Dean of International Studies and Programs
Michigan State University

David C. Prejsnar, Coordinator for International
Education and Professor of History and Philosophy
Community College of Philadelphia

Celeste Schenck, Professor of Comparative Literature
and Associate Dean for Curriculum Development
The American University of Paris

Alan Shulman, Director of International Projects
Office of Alternative, Adult and Continuing Education
New York Board of Education

Working Group on Civic Learning

Richard Battistoni, Professor of Political Science
Providence College

José Calderon, Professor of Sociology
Pitzer College

Walter E. Fluker, Director, The Leadership Center
Morehouse College

Robert Franco, Director of Planning and Institutional
Research
University of Hawai'i–Kapi'olani Community College

Elizabeth Minnich, Core Professor, Interdisciplinary
Studies
The Union Institute and University

Caryn McTighe Musil, cochair, Vice President for
Diversity, Equity, and Global Initiatives
AAC&U

Leigh Ann Orr, Teacher
Manual Arts High School, Los Angeles, California

Maria Trementozzi, Middle School Social Studies
Specialist
Montgomery County Public School, Maryland

Heather Wathington, cochair, Director of Programs
Office of Diversity, Equity, and Global Initiatives
AAC&U

* Affiliations at the time of the forum's work.

About the Authors

Andrea Leskes, president of the Institute for American Universities in Aix-en-Provence, France, was vice president for education and quality initiatives at the Association of American Colleges and Universities (AAC&U) from 1999 to 2006. She led the Greater Expectations initiative on the aims and best practices of undergraduate education for the twenty-first century and was the principal author of *Greater Expectations: A New Vision for Learning as a Nation Goes to College*. For six years, Leskes directed AAC&U's annual Institute on General Education; she writes regularly for the association's quarterly journals, and consults with campuses on curricular reform.

Leskes holds a PhD in cell biology from the Rockefeller University and an MA in French from the University of Massachusetts at Amherst. She formerly served as vice president for academic affairs and professor of comparative literature at the American University of Paris, vice provost for undergraduate education at Northeastern University, associate dean at Brandeis University, and assistant dean at Dartmouth College.

Ross Miller joined AAC&U in 1999, as director of programs for the Office of Education and Quality Initiatives, to assist in the planning and implementation of the Greater Expectations initiative. He is also assistant director of the AAC&U Institute on General Education.

Miller holds a BM and MM in trumpet performance from the University of Michigan and an EdD in music education from the University of Illinois. During his thirteen years at Nazareth College (Rochester, New York), he taught both undergraduate and graduate music education students while also serving as director of the graduate program. In an assignment as Nazareth's assessment coordinator, Miller was responsible for assessment of the college's general education program. He has served as a question writer in the arts for the National Assessment of Educational Progress and worked on a team developing a high school outcomes test in the arts for the New York State Education Department. ■